3Kiddos Publishing
Just Painted Rocks


Created by Aimee Schneider

Distributed In Partnership With
3Kiddos Publishing



www.3kiddospublishing.com

ISBN:
978-1-969926-07-5

# DEDICATION

THIS IS DEDICATED TO RANDY, ANDREW, AND MACKENZIE-MY CONSTANT SUPPORT, MY BIGGEST CHEERLEADERS, AND MY REASON FOR CONTINUING TO DREAM AND CREATE. YOUR LOVE, PATIENCE, AND ENCOURAGEMENT MEAN MORE TO ME THAN WORDS COULD EVER EXPRESS.

TO MY BIG BROTHERS, JON AND JEFF-ALTHOUGH WE DIDN'T GROW UP SIDE BY SIDE, YOU HAVE ALWAYS BEEN TWO PEOPLE I DEEPLY ADMIRE AND LOOK UP TO. YOUR SUPPORT, GUIDANCE, AND BELIEF IN ME HAVE MEANT MORE TO ME THAN YOU KNOW.

TO CHELSEY-NONE OF THIS WOULD HAVE BEEN POSSIBLE WITHOUT YOU. YOUR BELIEF IN ME, YOUR ENCOURAGEMENT, AND THE TIME, ENERGY, AND HEART YOU'VE POURED INTO THIS JOURNEY MEAN MORE THAN I CAN EVER EXPLAIN. WHAT STARTED AS A SHARED IDEA TURNED INTO SOMETHING SO MUCH BIGGER, AND ALONG THE WAY YOU BECAME MY BEST FRIEND. I AM ENDLESSLY GRATEFUL FOR YOU AND FOR EVERYTHING WE'VE BUILT TOGETHER.

AND TO MY MOM BARB, MY DAD RICK, AND MY AUNTY CANDY-WATCHING FROM HEAVEN. I KNOW YOU WOULD BE SO PROUD OF HOW FAR I'VE COME AND THE NEW JOURNEYS I'M TAKING IN LIFE. THANK YOU FOR WATCHING OVER MY FAMILY AND SURROUNDING US WITH LOVE.

THIS DEDICATION IS FOR ALL OF YOU-PAST AND PRESENT-WHO CONTINUE TO GUIDE ME, INSPIRE ME, AND WALK WITH ME THROUGH EVERY NEW CHAPTER OF LIFE.

*Just Aimee*

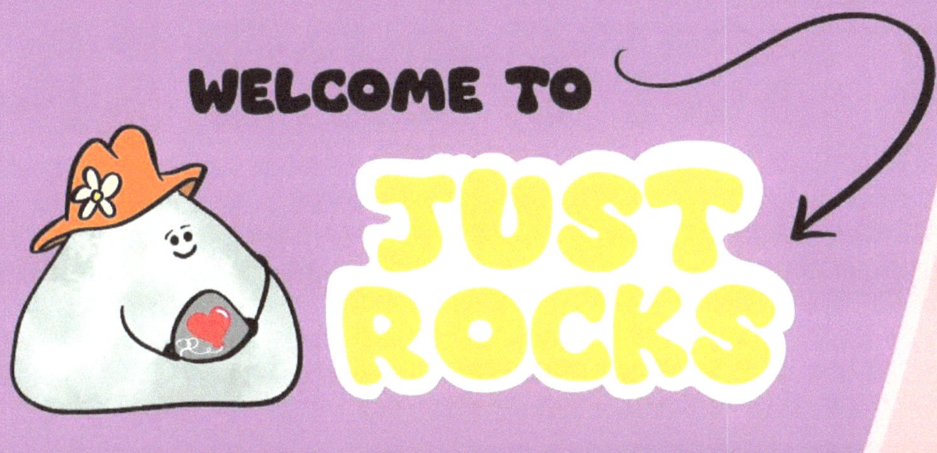


A CREATIVE, KIND-HEARTED COMMUNITY
INSPIRED BY OUR LOVE
FOR PAINTING, SHARING,
AND CONNECTING THROUGH ART. 🎨💫

WHAT STARTED AS A LOCAL KINDNESS
ROCKS PROJECT HAS GROWN INTO
SOMETHING SO MUCH MORE -

A PLACE WHERE
EVERY ROCK TELLS A STORY
AND EVERY ARTIST
(NO MATTER YOUR SKILL LEVEL!)
BELONGS.

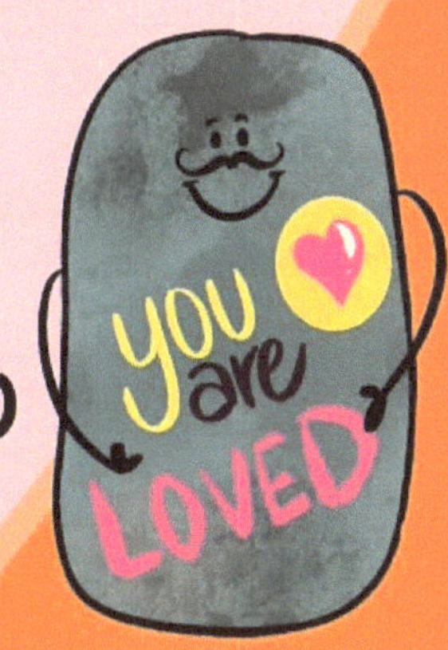


HERE YOU'LL FIND:

🎨 INSPIRATION, TIPS, AND ENCOURAGEMENT
FOR PAINTERS OF ALL AGES

📚 STEP BY STEP INSPIRATIO

📸 UNEDITED PHOTOS OF
REAL LIFE PAINTED ROCKS

# OUR SUPPORTERS

"WE EXTEND OUR DEEPEST GRATITUDE TO THE DICKINSON COUNTY BUSINESSES THAT STEPPED FORWARD TO CHAMPION THIS PROJECT. BY DONATING WITH YOUR HEARTS, YOU HAVE NOT ONLY BROUGHT THE JUST ROCKS GLOBAL CATALOG TO LIFE BUT HAVE ALSO FUELED A MISSION OF CONNECTION AND CREATIVITY THAT REACHES FAR BEYOND OUR LOCAL BORDERS.
YOUR GENEROSITY ENSURES THAT THIS LEGACY OF KINDNESS TRAVELS FROM OUR COMMUNITY TO THE WORLD, AND WE ARE HONORED TO CARRY YOUR NAMES WITHIN THESE PAGES AS PARTNERS IN THIS JOURNEY."

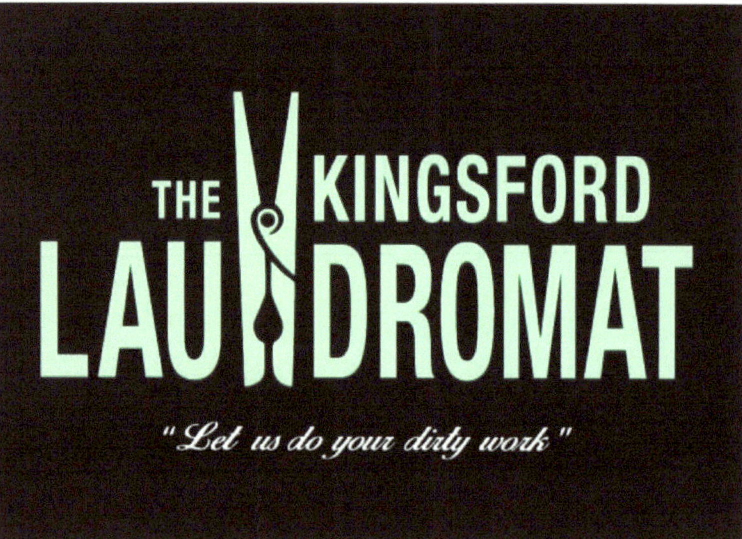


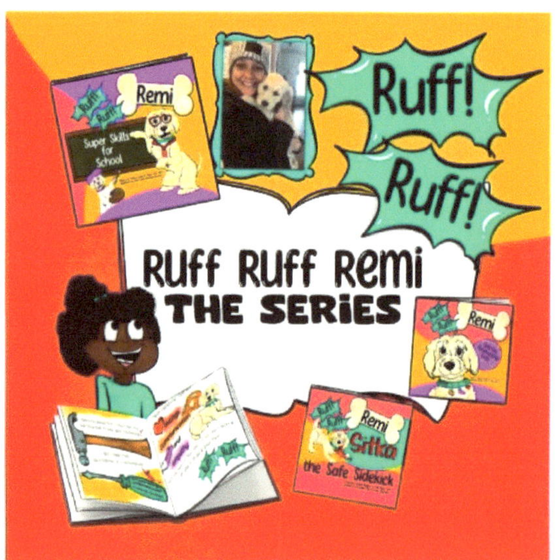


DANIELSON INSURANCE GROUP:

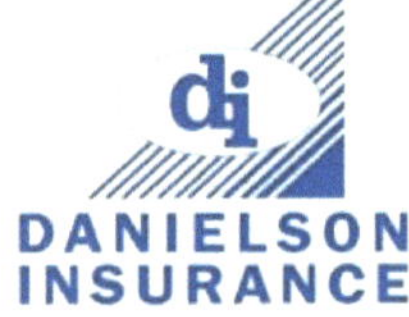


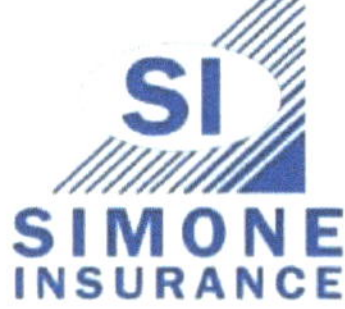


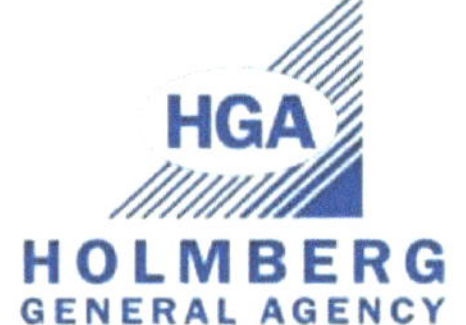


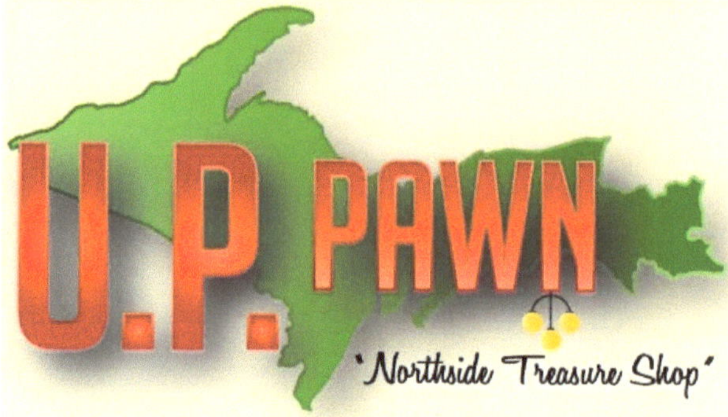


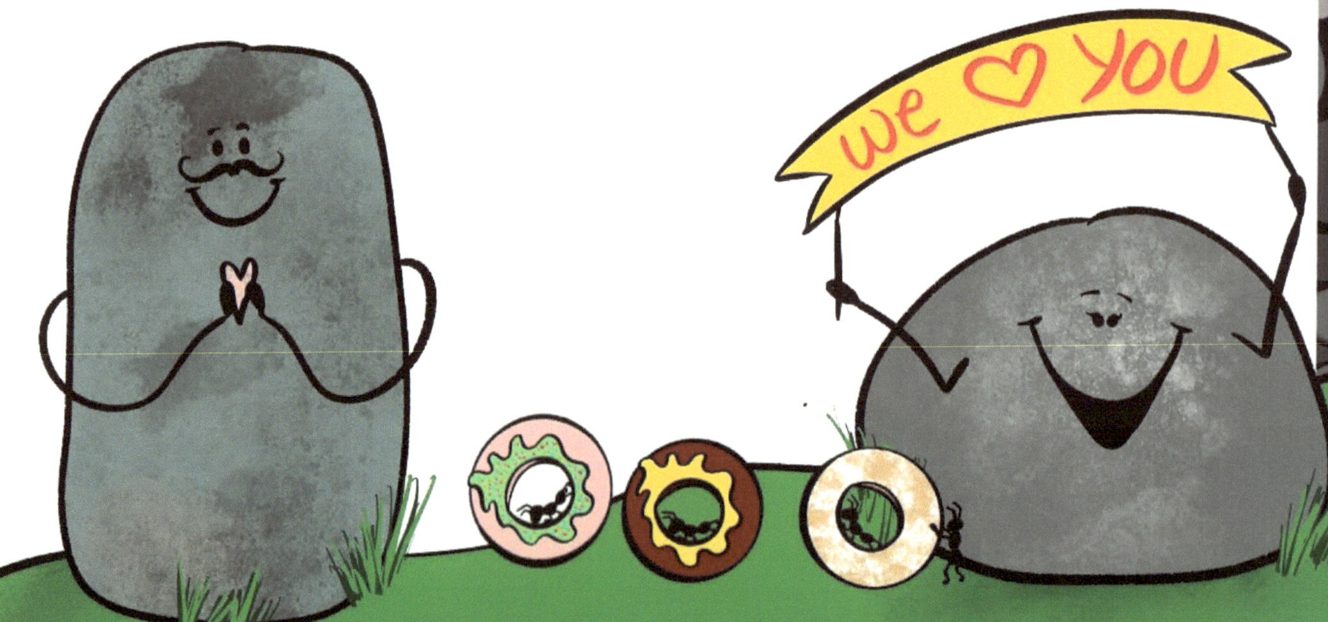

Meet the Rocker 2025

# JUST AIMEE

● Mother ● Crafter ● Iggy ● Rocker

31,October 2025

## A HOBBY THAT KEPT ON ROCKIN'

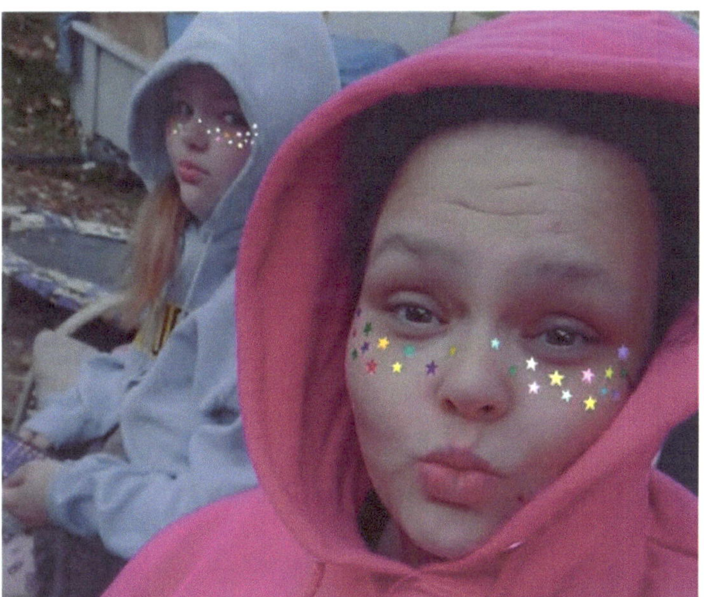

I dont even know where to start! I do know that this has expanded into so much more than I ever thought it was going but WOW I'm so glad it did! I have been contemplating painting rocks for a while, and one day we went by the river and we found some gorgeous rocks and i immediately knew i wanted to try painting rocks! And my gosh the rest is history and it has literally not even been a full month and holy smokes! We're sharing stories, writing books, painting rocks, doing events at the library, making friends and seriously living our best lives!

Im a stay-at-home mom to a very energetic 5 year old son and a 15 year old daughter! They both love rock painting! We find the perfect rocks together, paint together and do rock drops together! We made it a family thing and we enough it so much! I honestly wantes a new hobby to try with my hubby and kiddos!

Rock painting has brought this amazing community together and i can't wait to see this book around for years to come! And I hope it puts a smile on your face! Like it did ours ! Thank you for being a part of something so great!

Written By: Aimee Jean

***"We are truly spreading kindness one rock at a time. We really did create something great and I couldn't have done it without you guys." -Aimee Schneider***

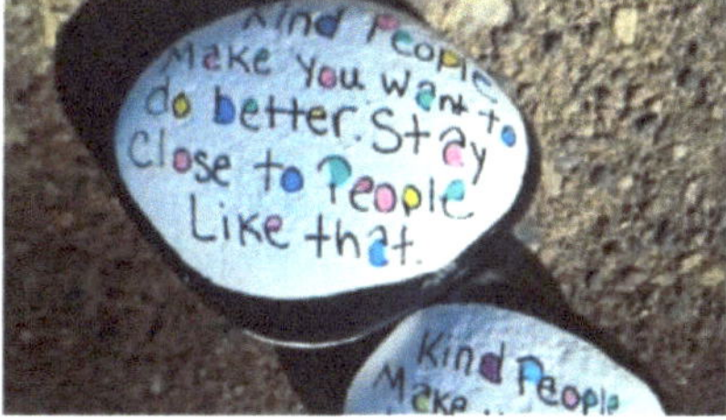


### Some tips and tricks I have are...

1. Spray painting your rocks first!! Makes them shine so nice!
2. Use a good clear coat! Also makes it shine!( I see a pattern here haha)
3.nail polish if fun to use too! I like using the glitter!
4. Never forget this is supposed to be fun! Not stress you out! You would be surprised what you can draw on a rock! Im no artist by any means and ive even surprised myself haha
5. I use all sorts of different acrylic markers!! I get them off Amazon and at walmart!

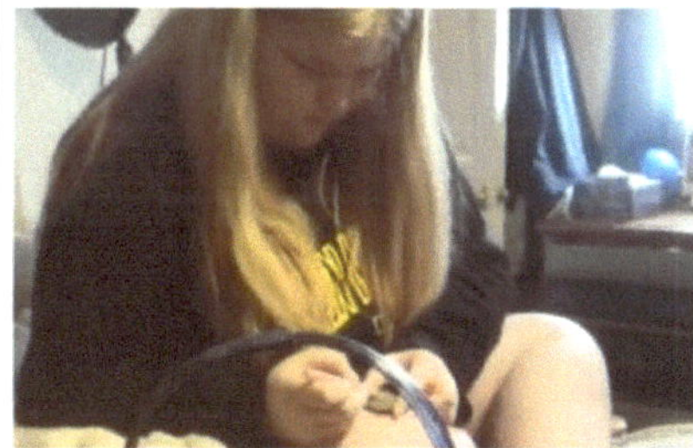

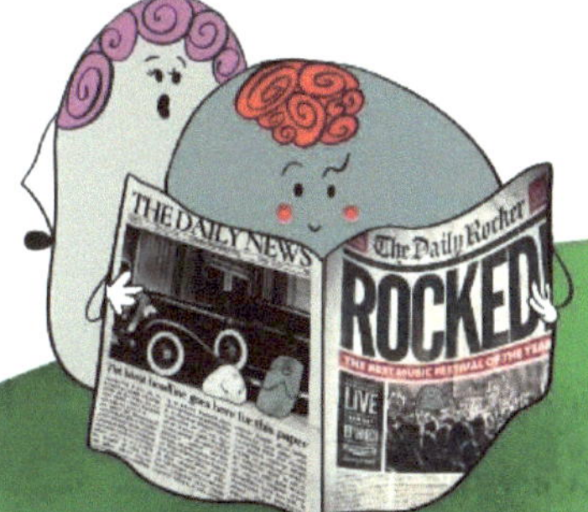

# STEP BY STEP

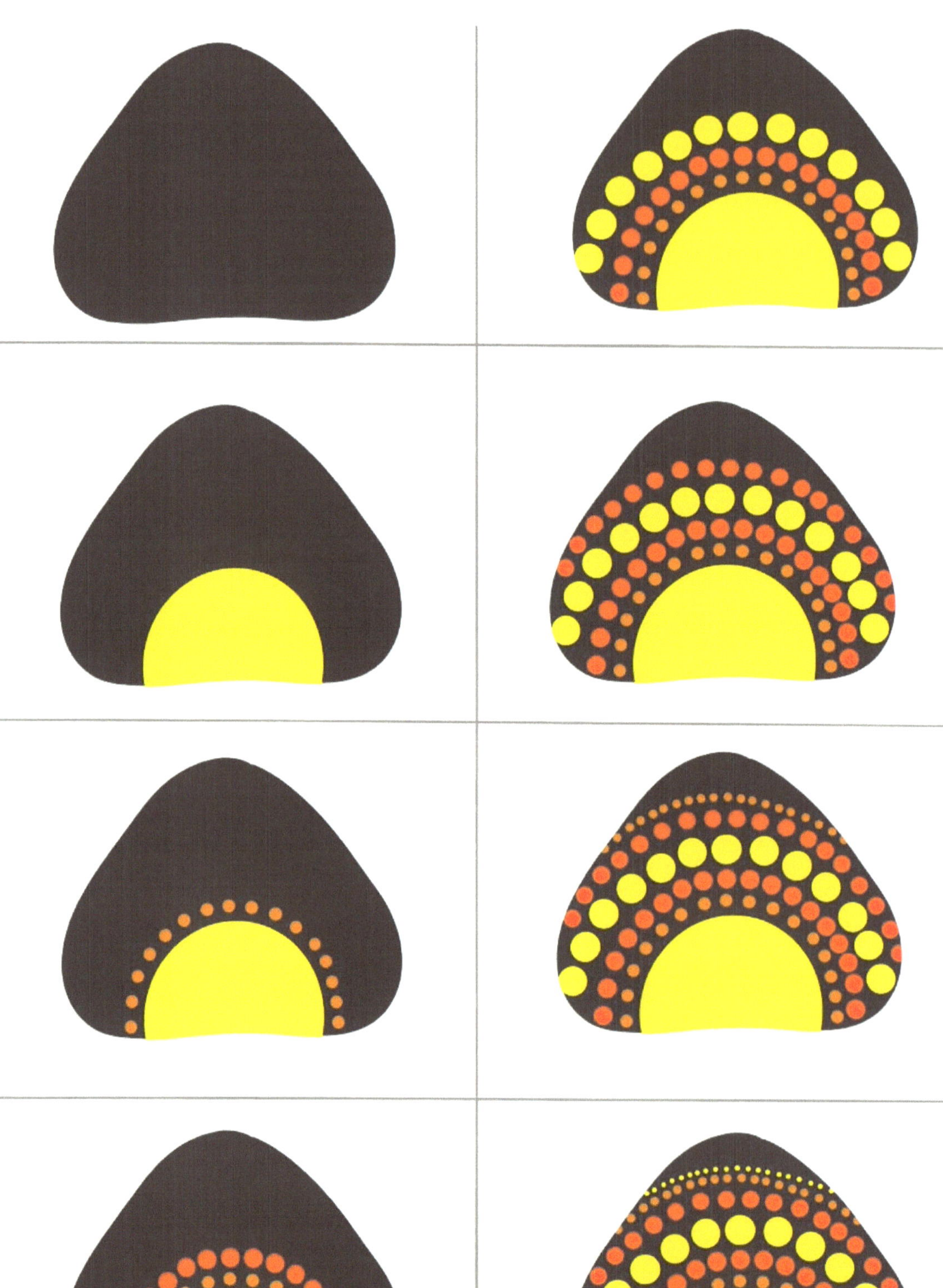

# STEP BY STEP

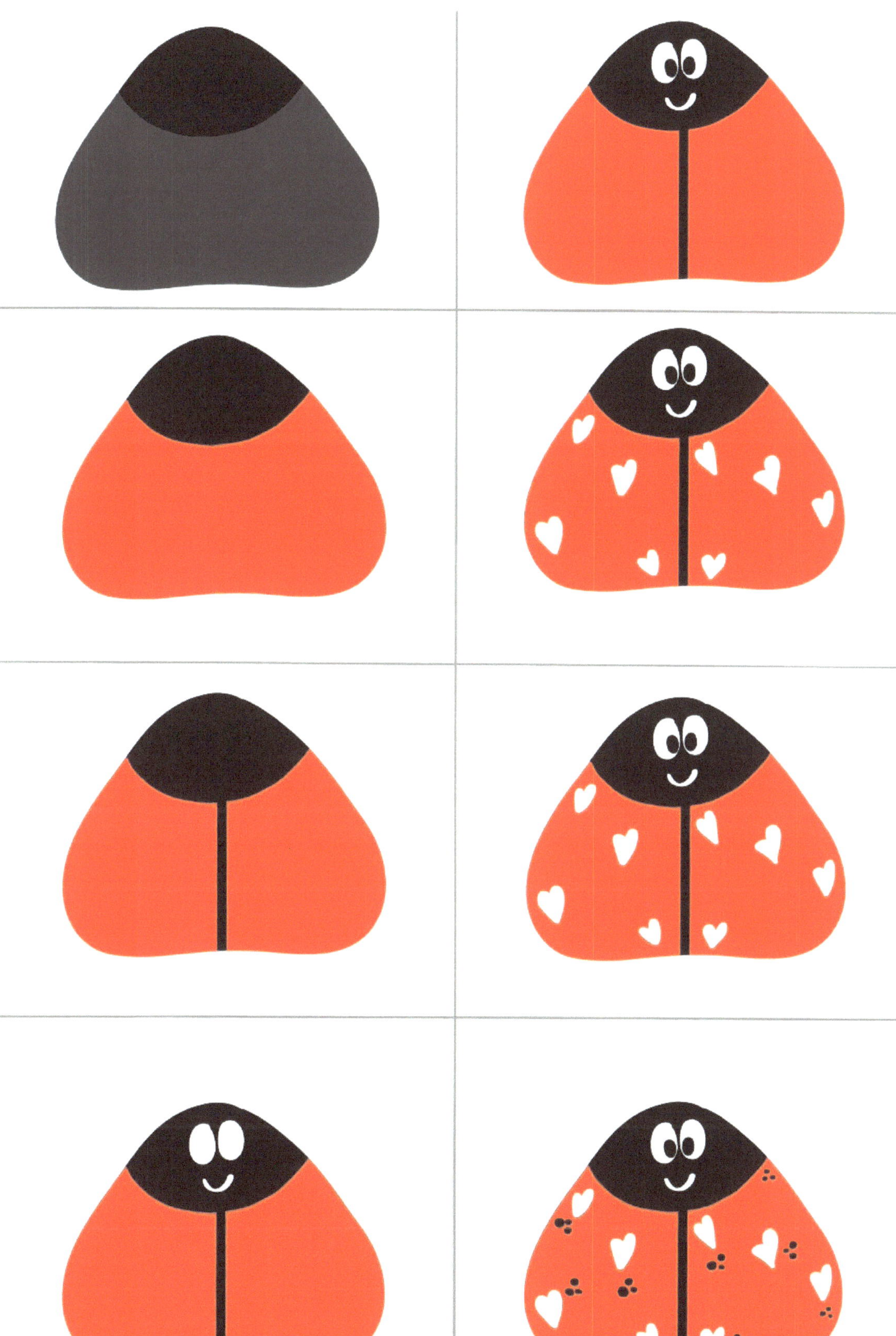

# STEP BY STEP

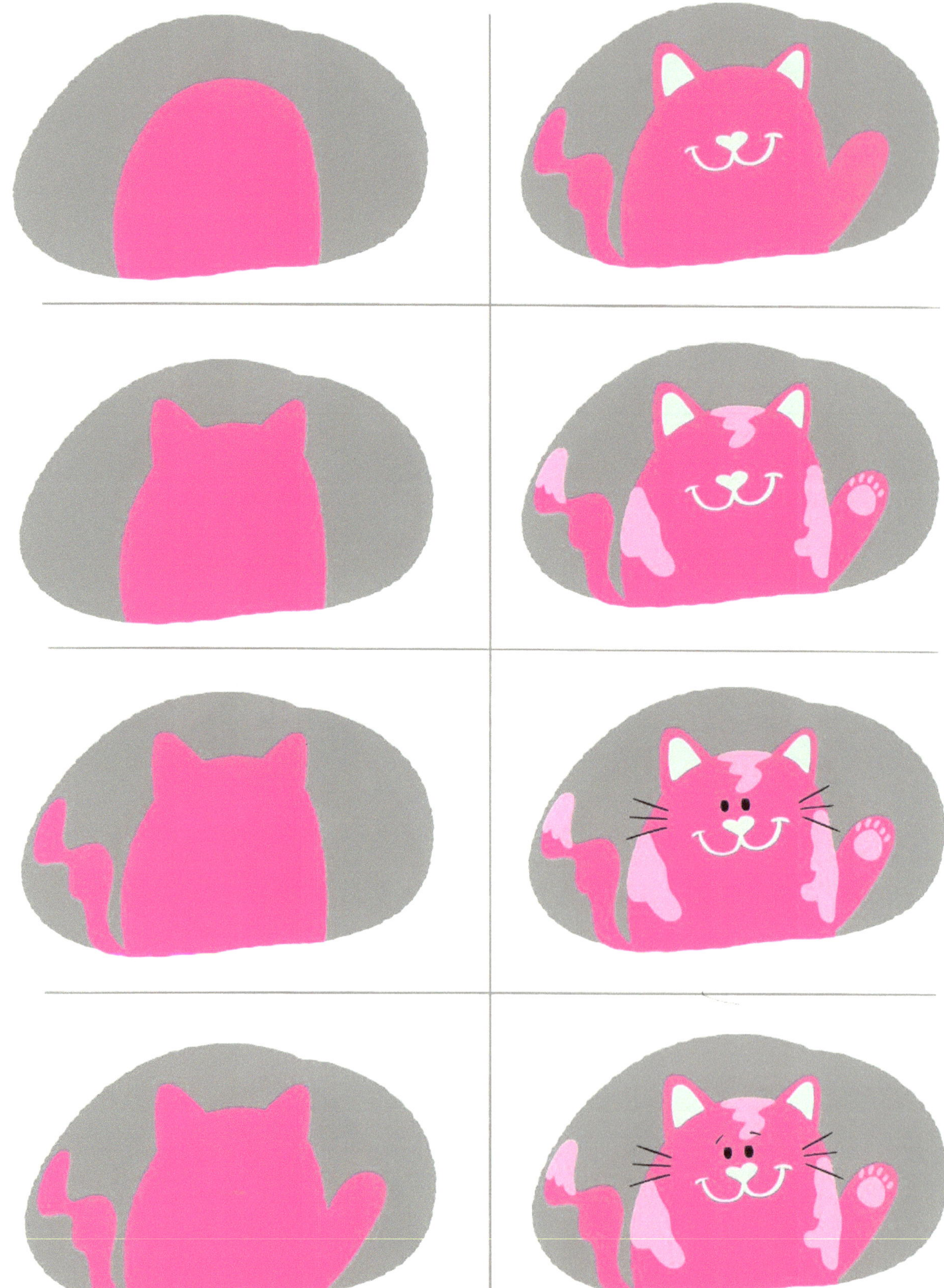

# STEP BY STEP

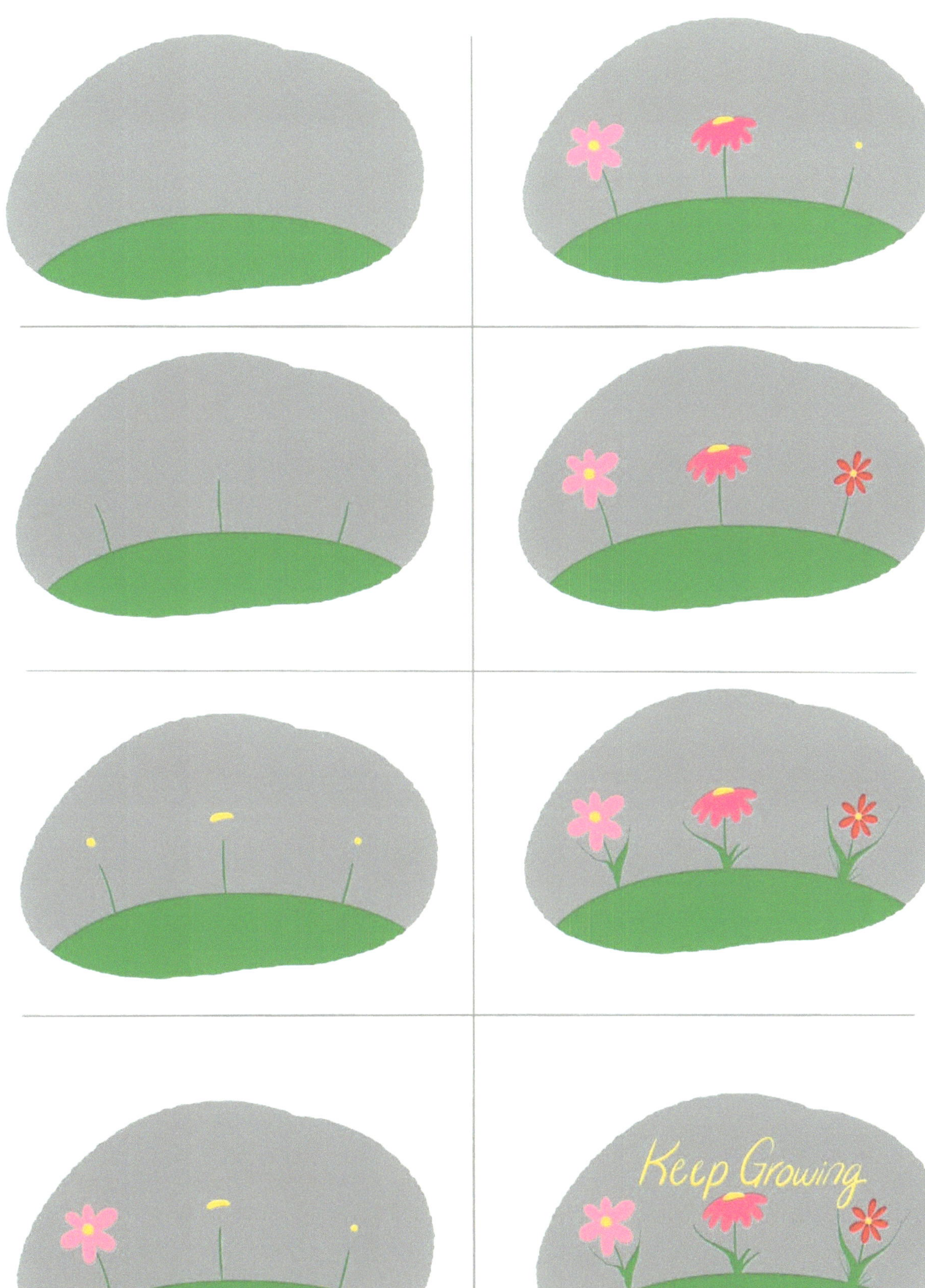

# STEP BY STEP

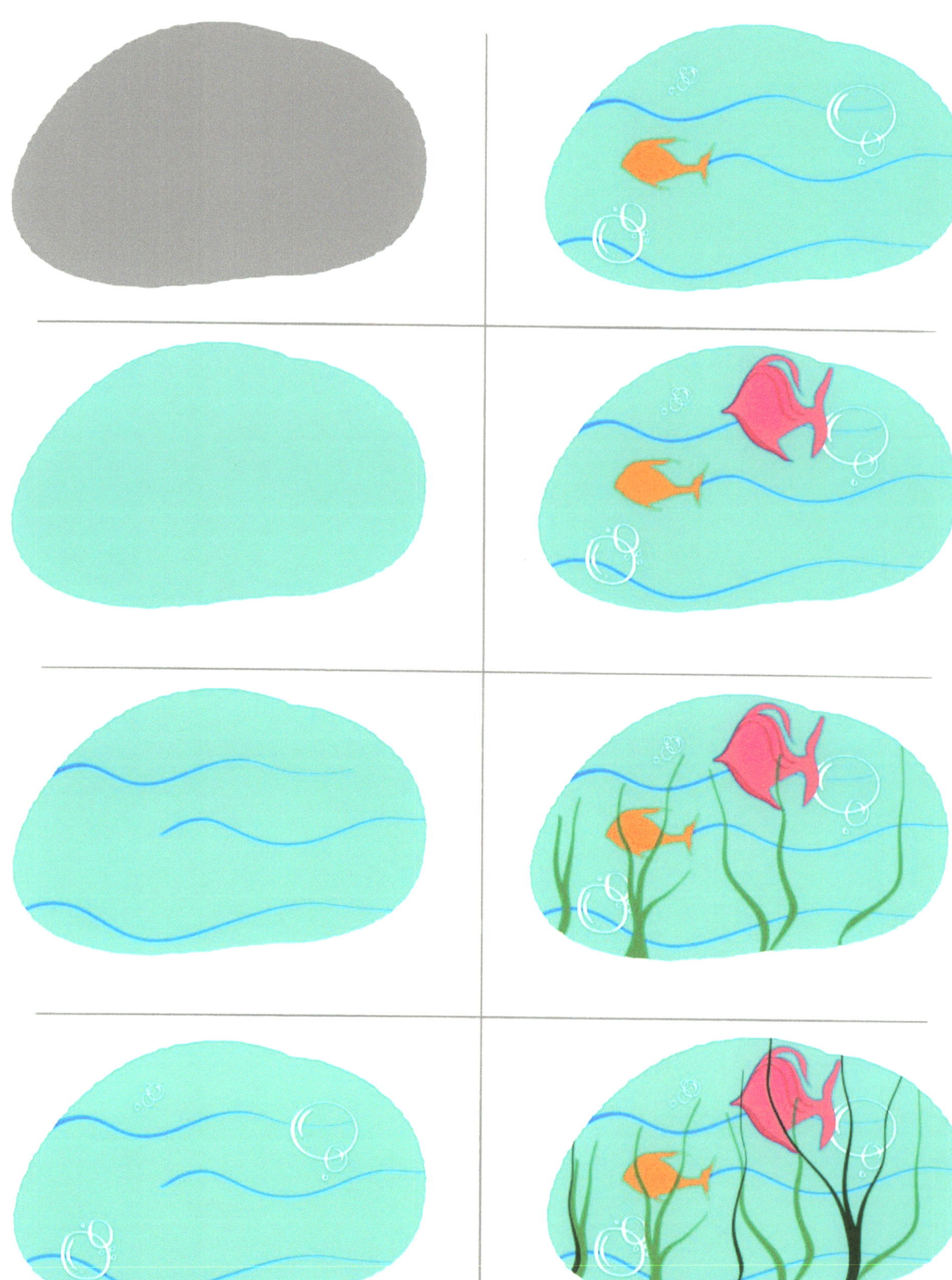

# STEP BY STEP

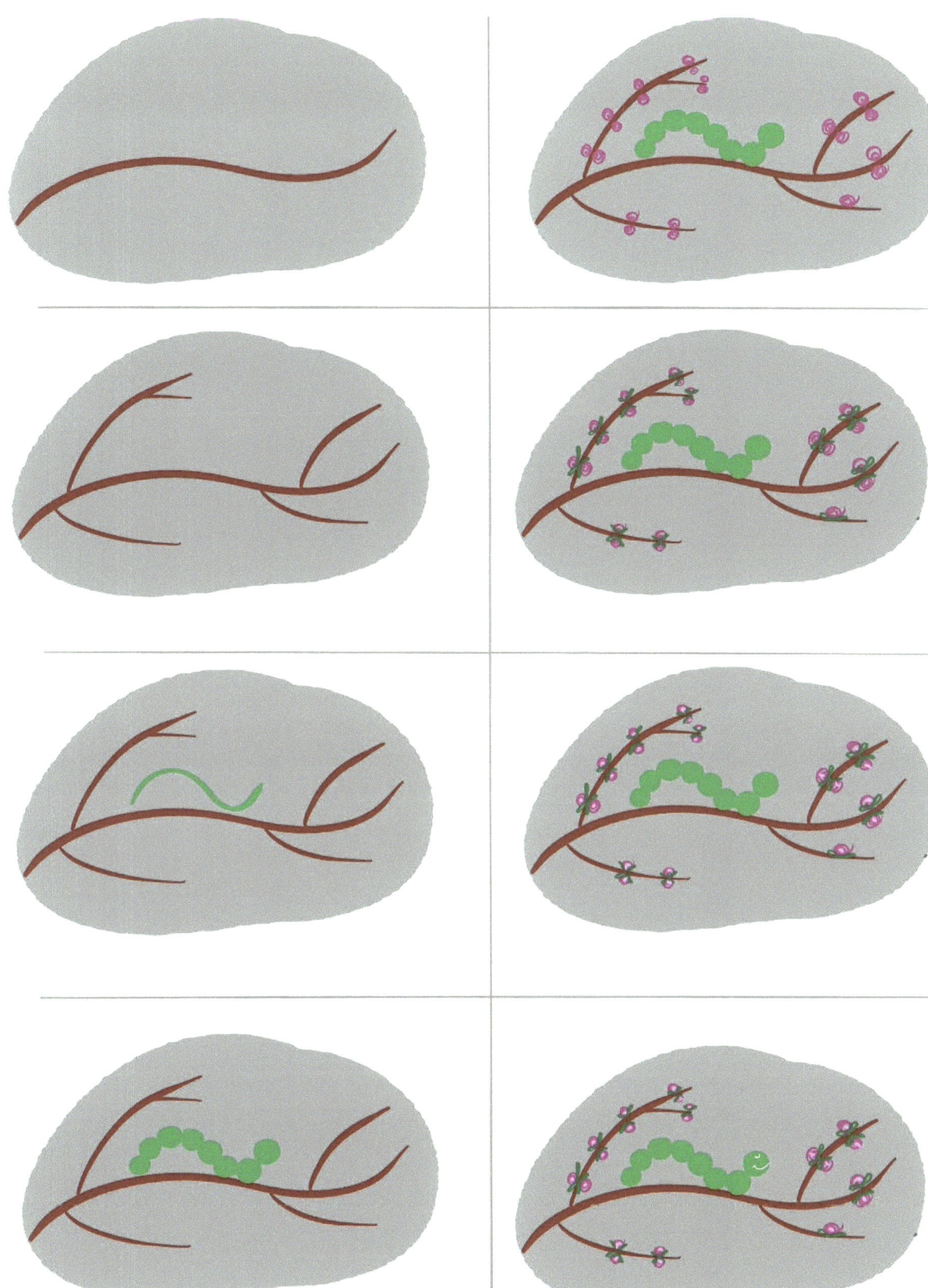

# STEP BY STEP

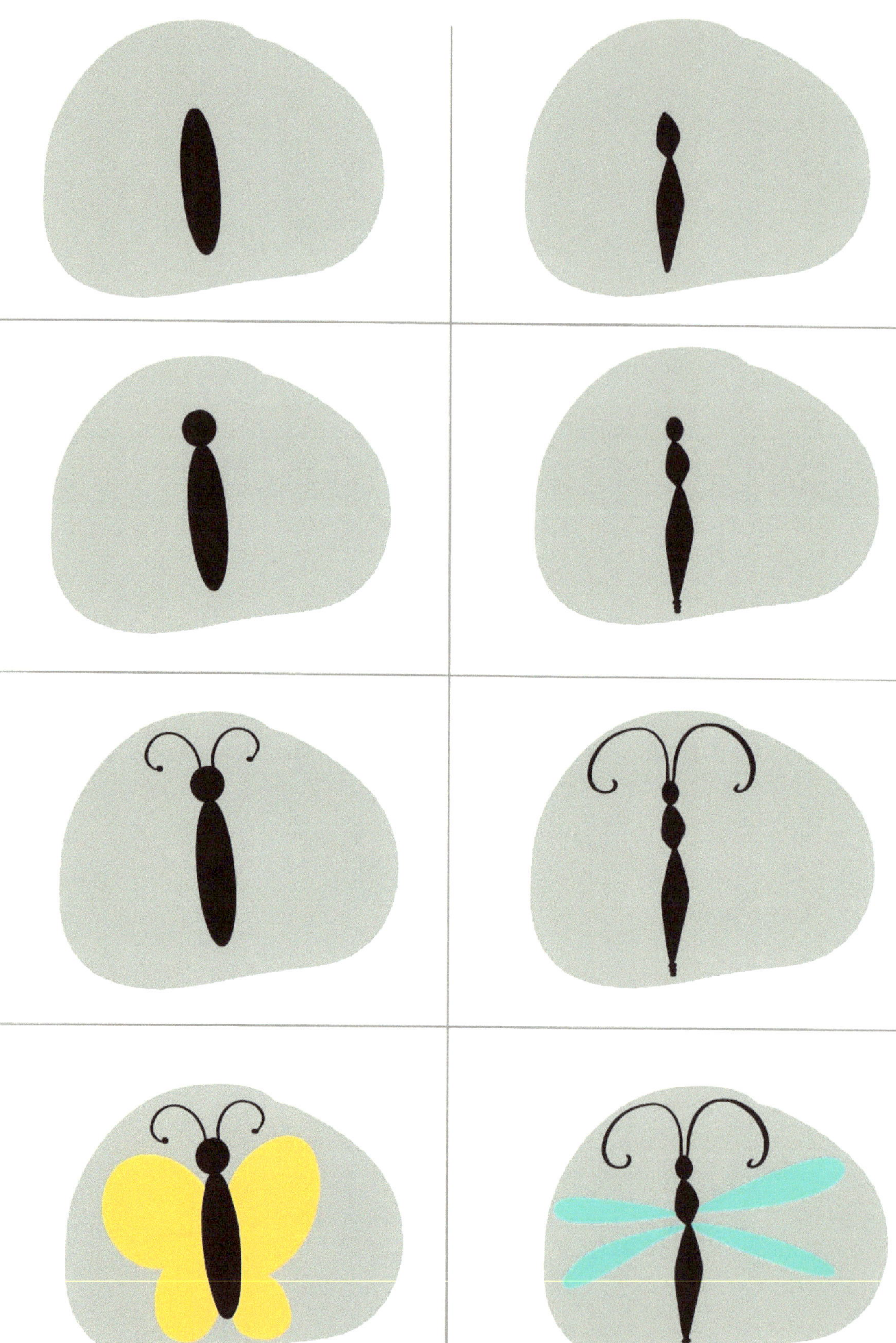

# STEP BY STEP

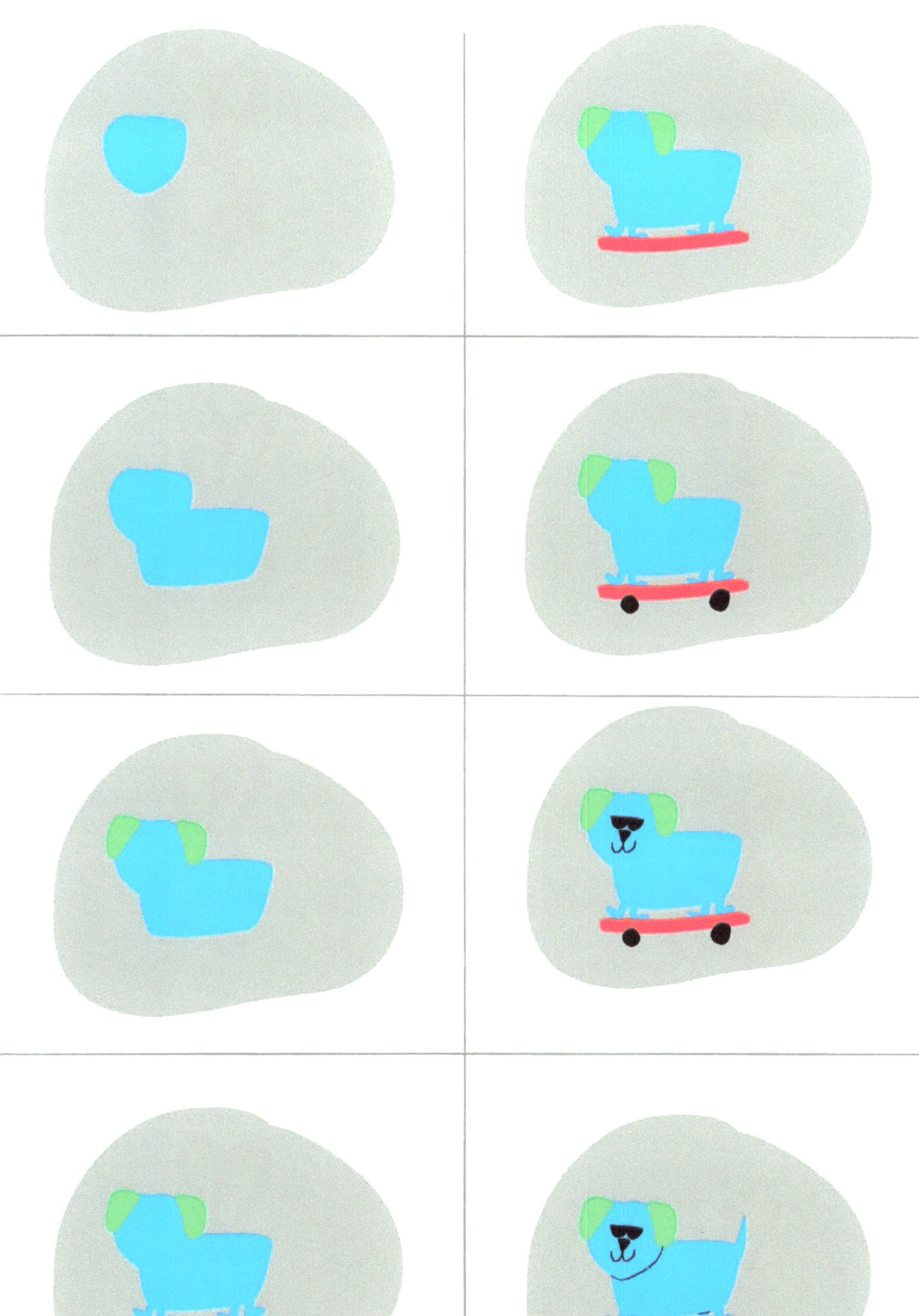

# STEP BY STEP

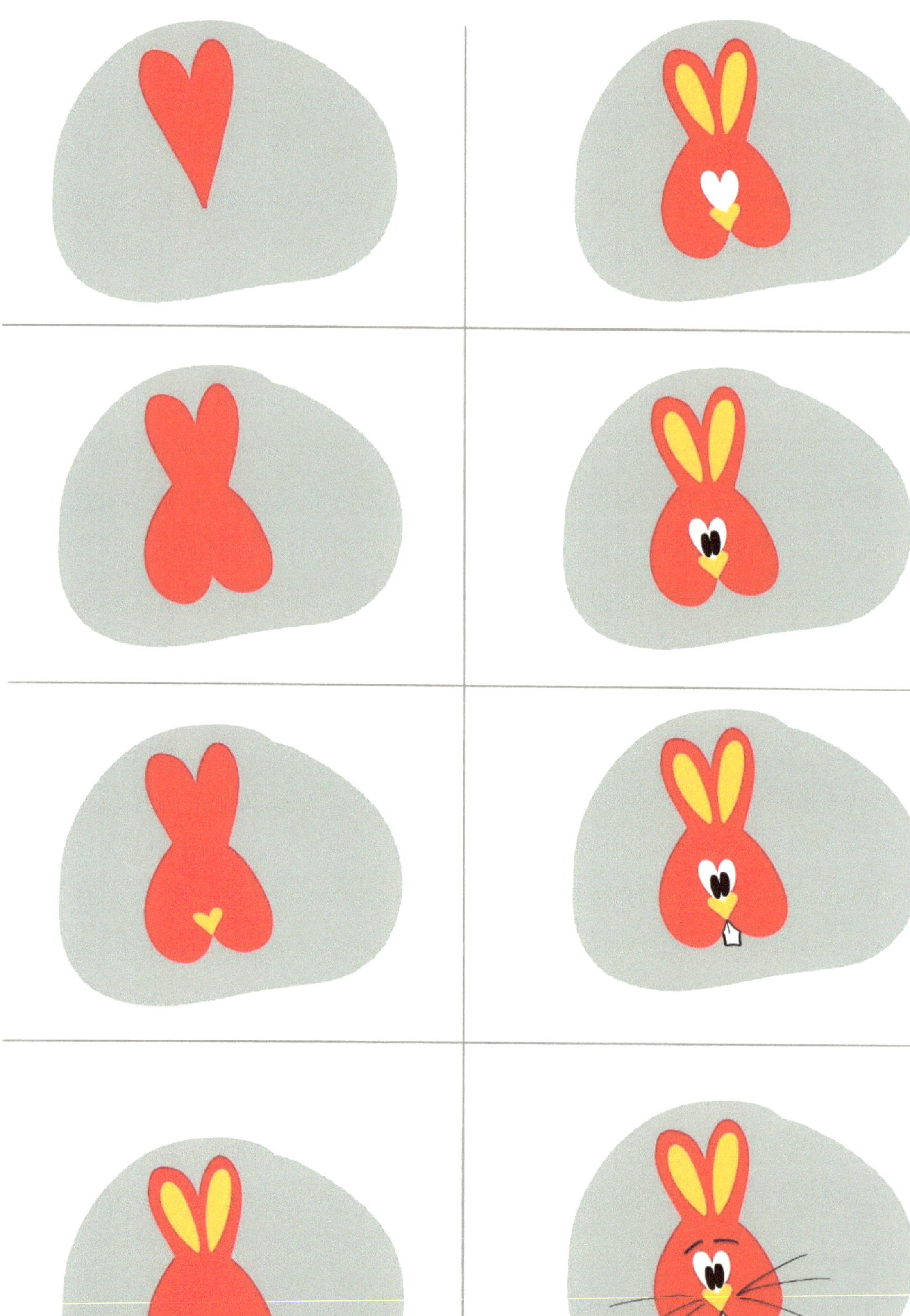

# CREATE WITH PATTERNS

WHEN ROCKS ARE ODDLY SHAPED, PATTERNS ARE A GREAT WAY TO NAVIGATE THE LUMPS AND BUMPS.

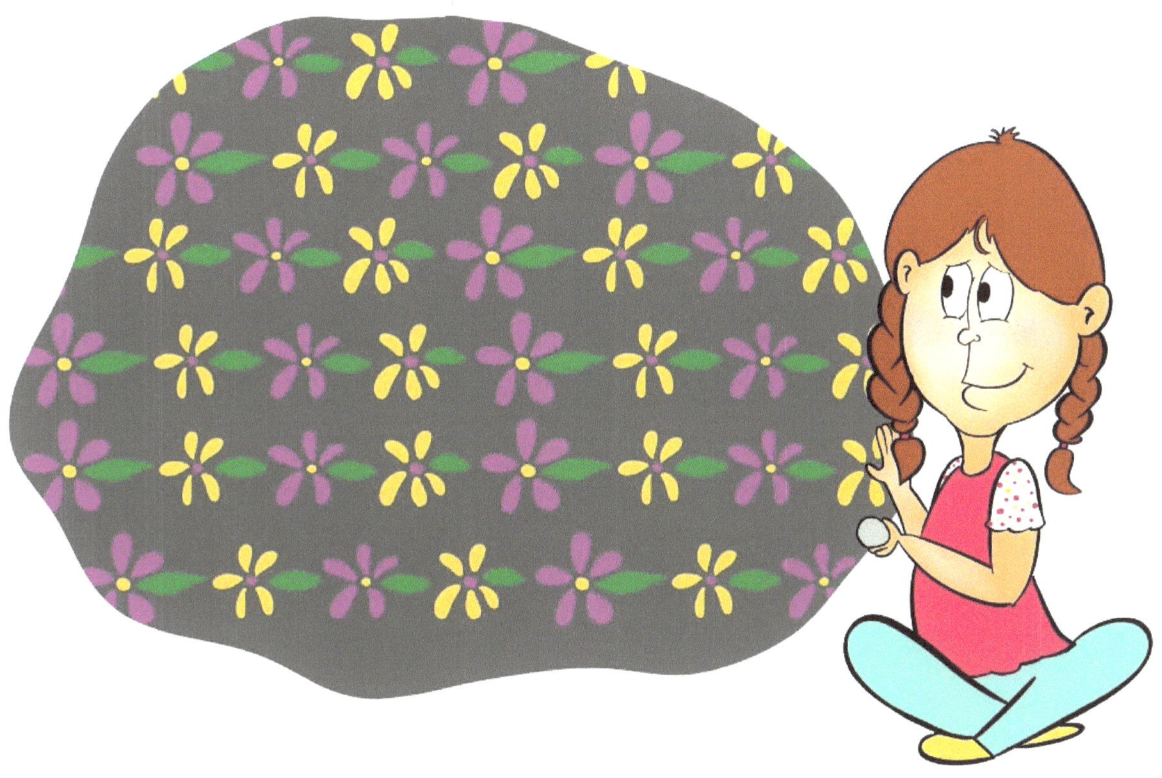

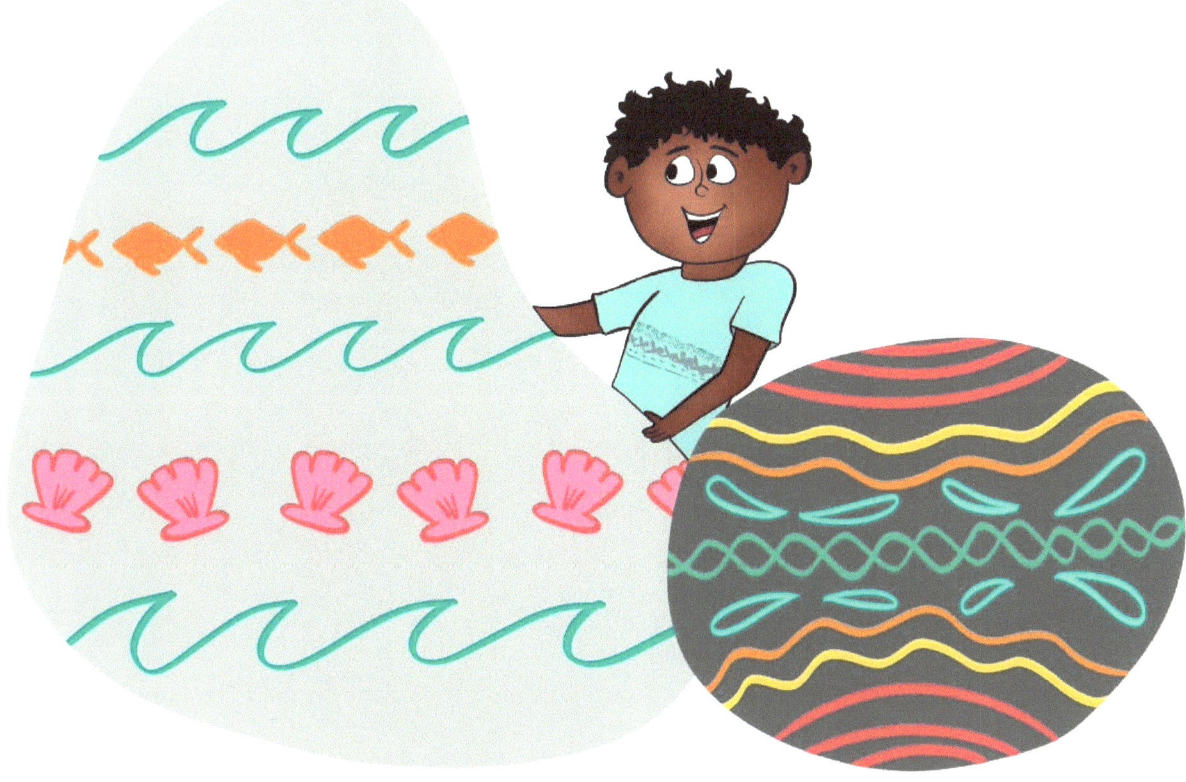

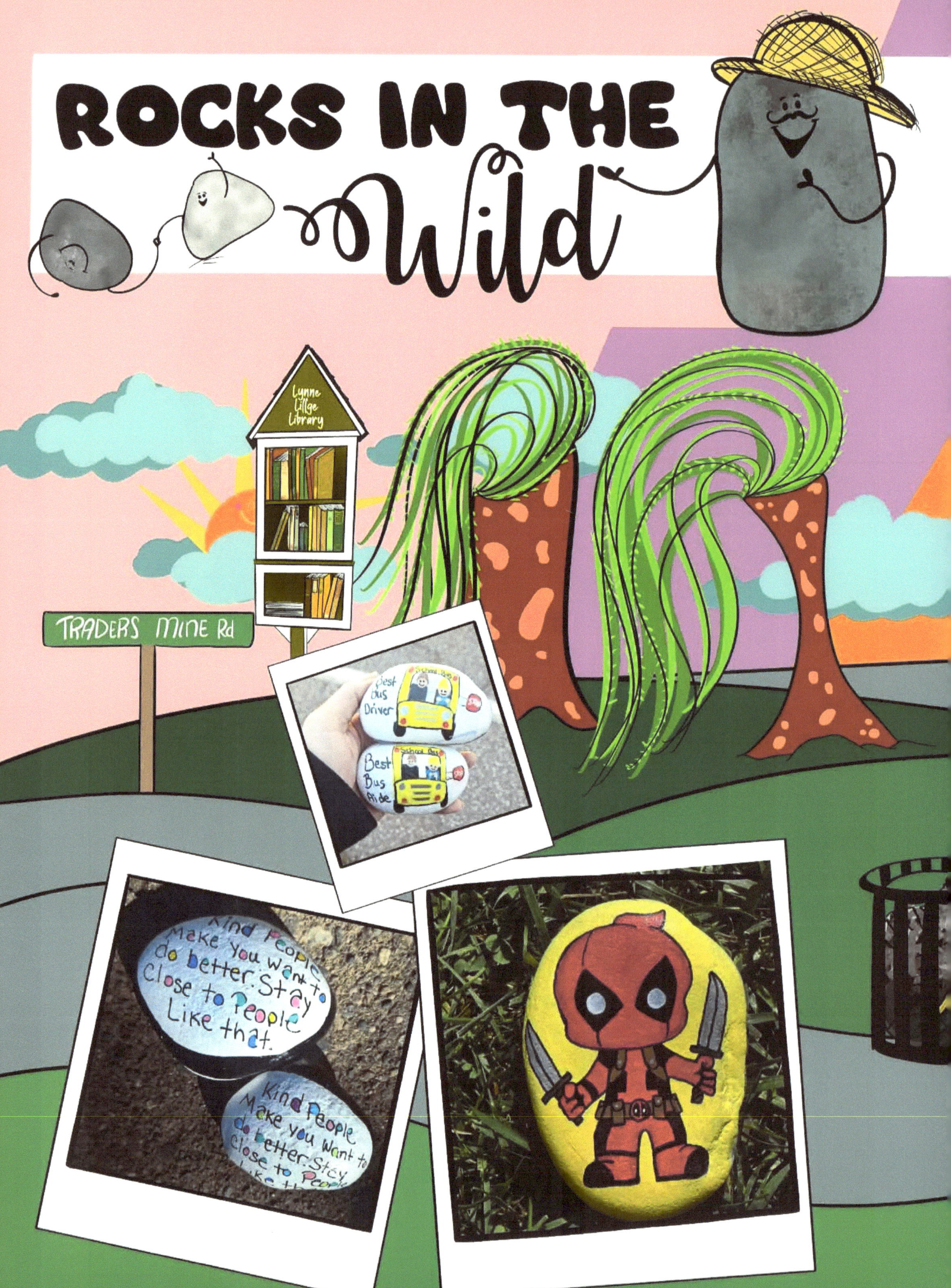
ROCKS IN THE
Wild
Lynne Lillge Library
TRADERS MINE Rd
Best Bus Driver
School Bus
STOP
Best Bus Ride
Kind People Make You want to do better. Stay close to People Like that.
Kind People Make you Want to do better. Stay close to People

**TIP:**
**MAKE SURE YOUR ROCKS HAVE A HELPFUL HIDING SPOT. WE DON'T WANT TO LEAVE ROCKS IN UNKNOWING YARDS.**

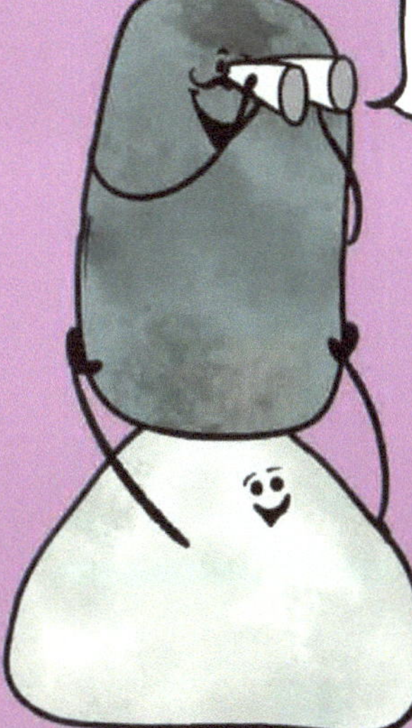

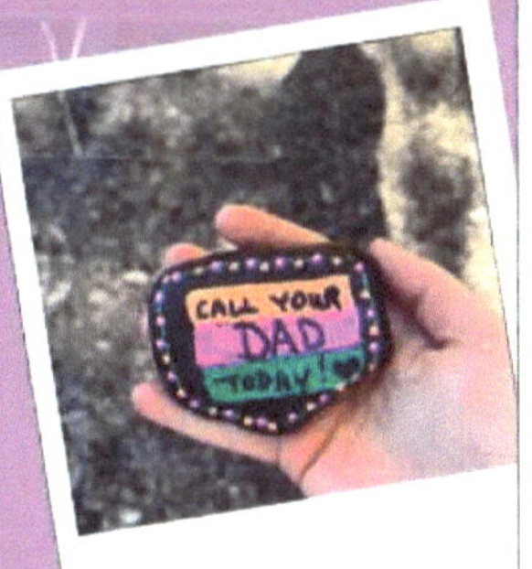


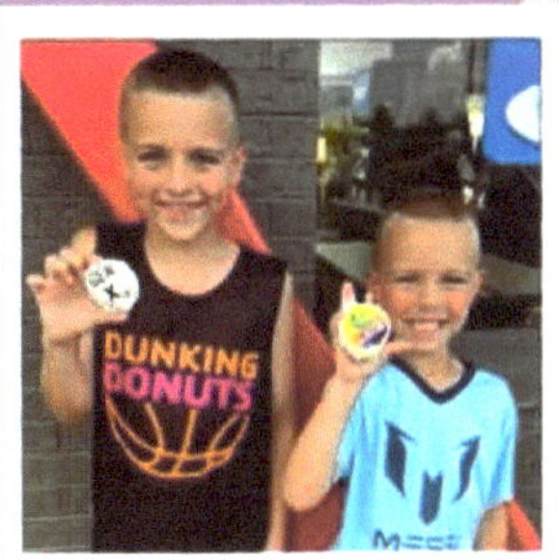


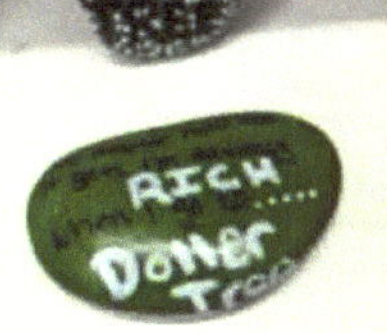


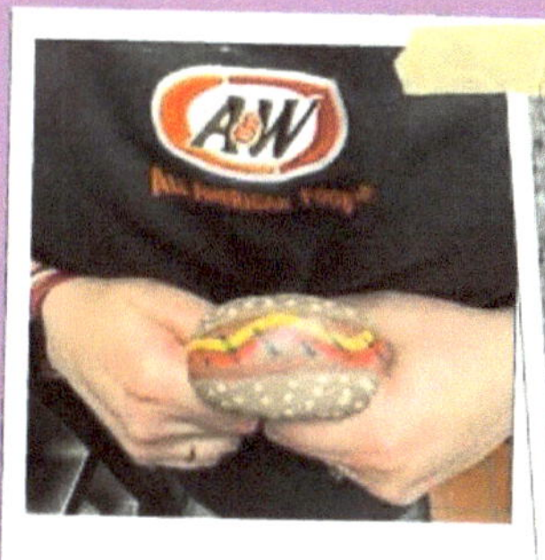


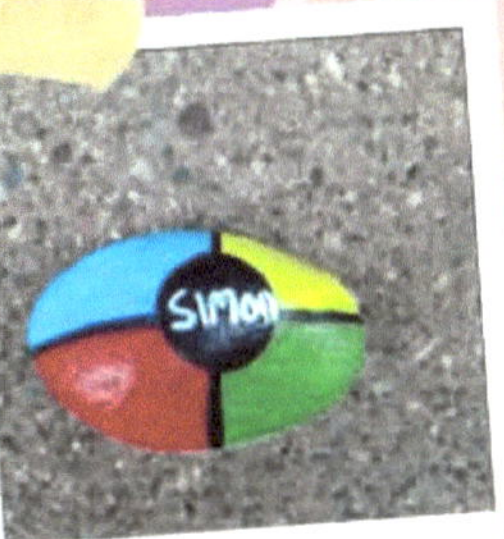


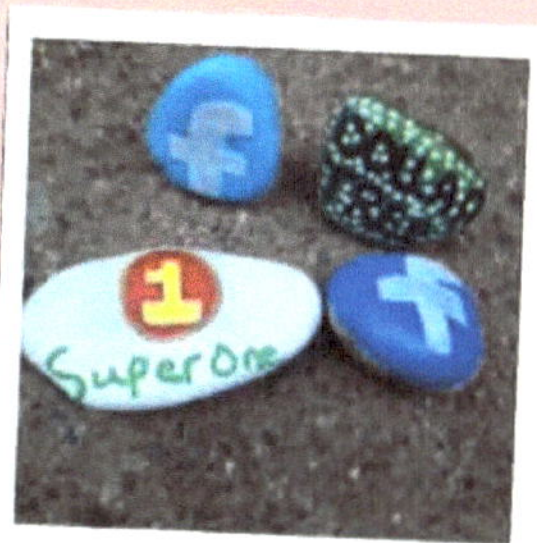


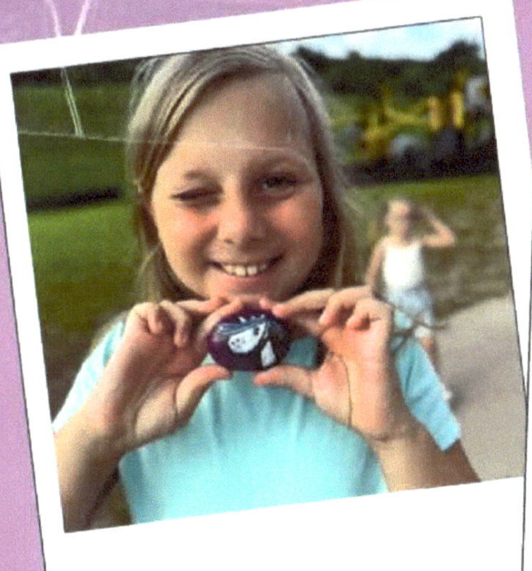

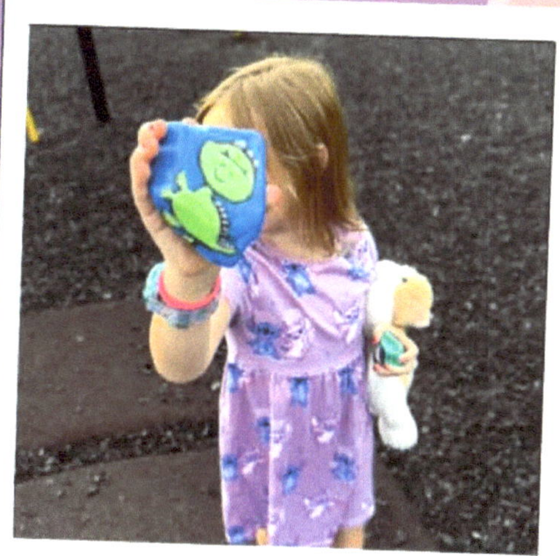

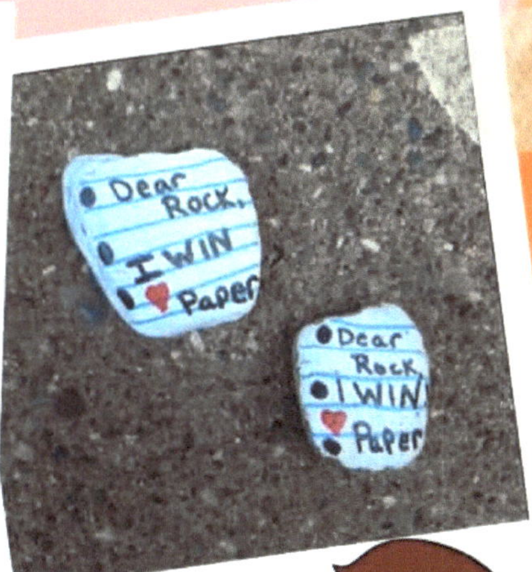


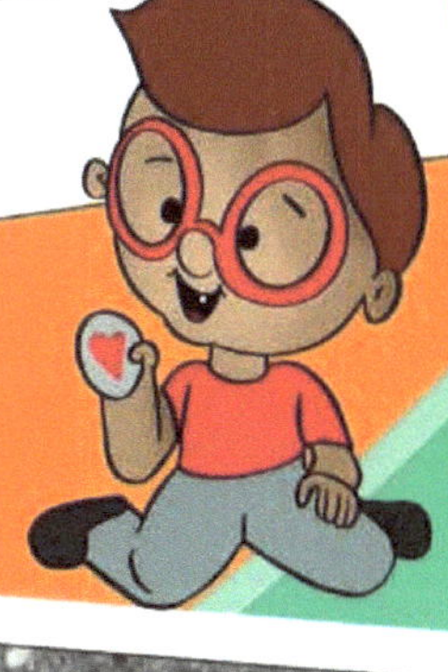

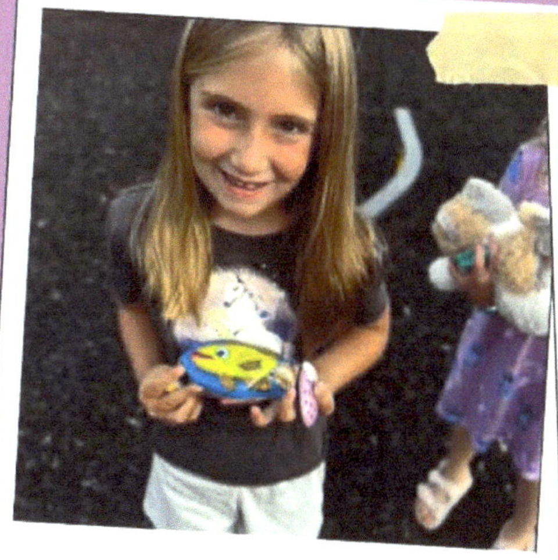

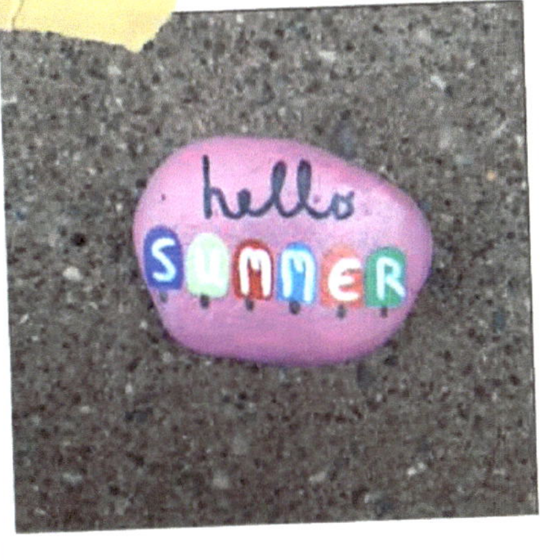


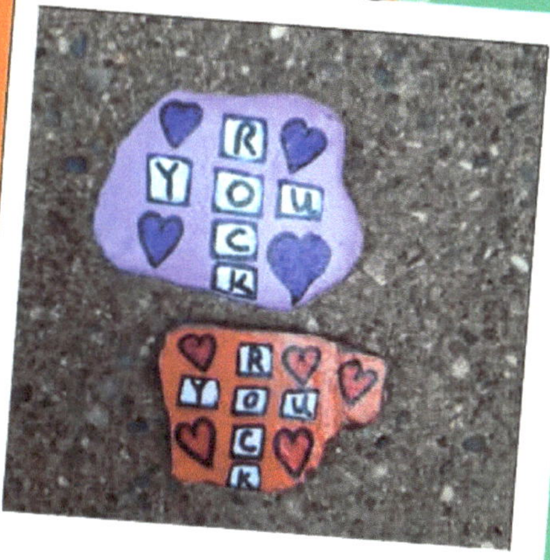

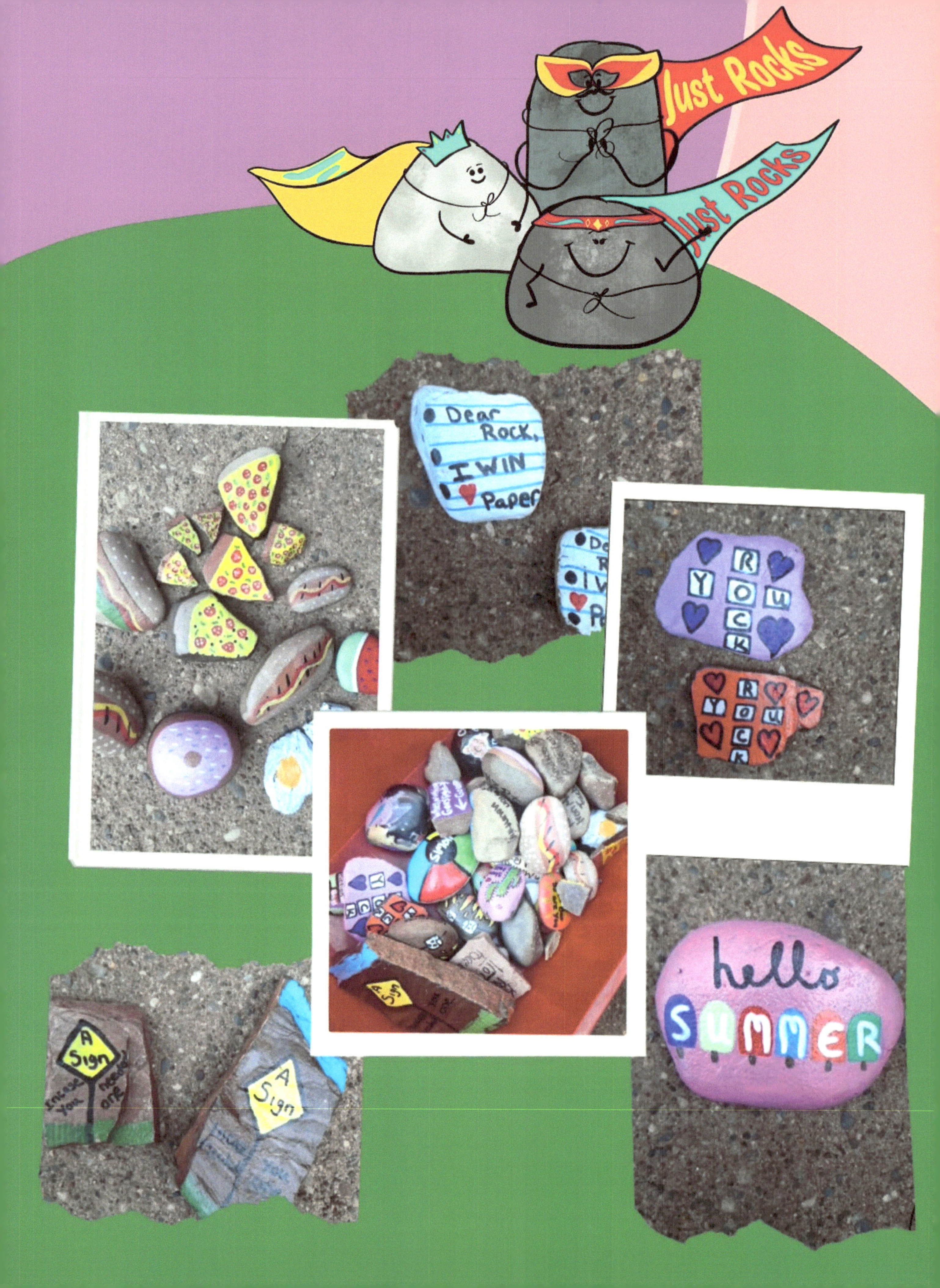

Just Rocks

Just Rocks

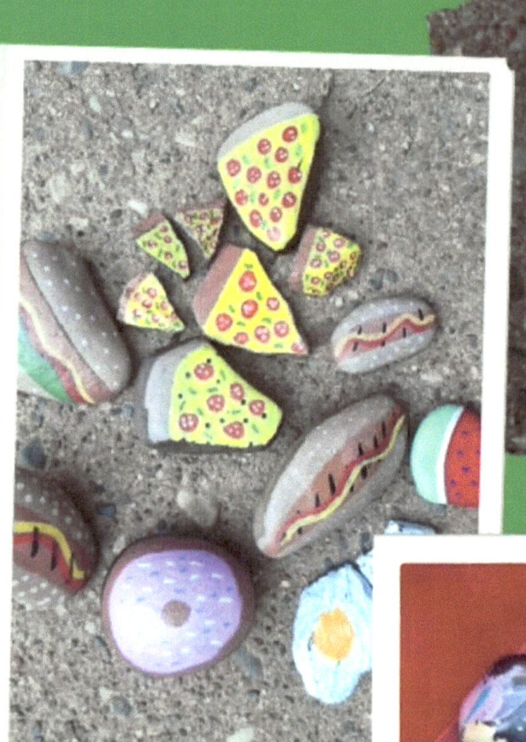

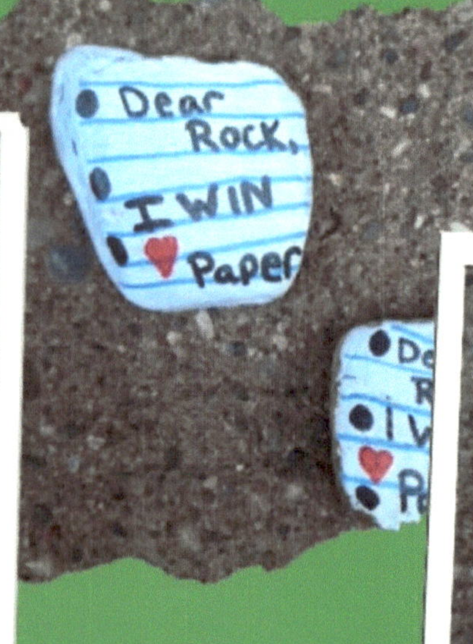


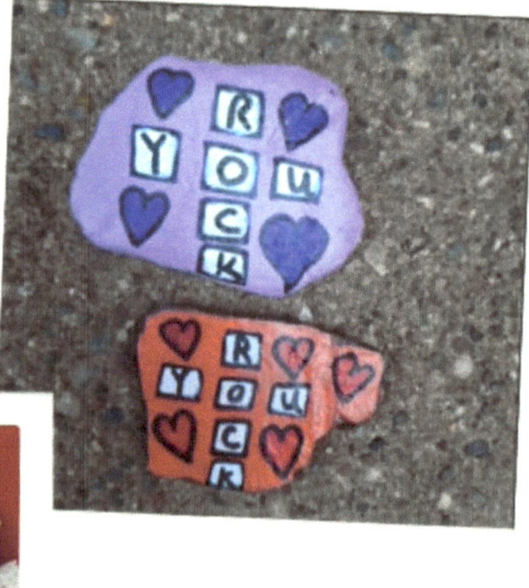


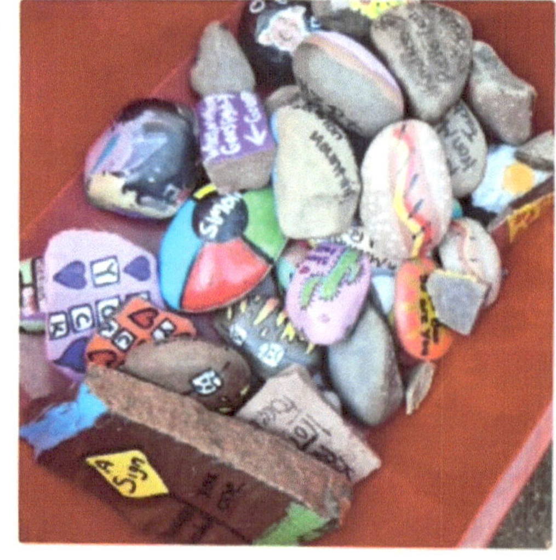


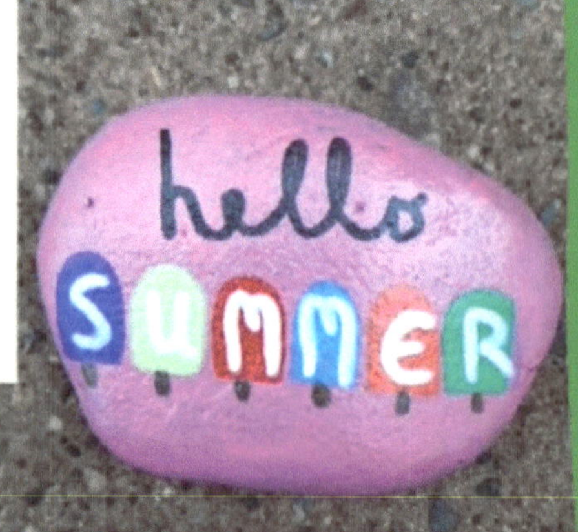


A Sign

A Sign

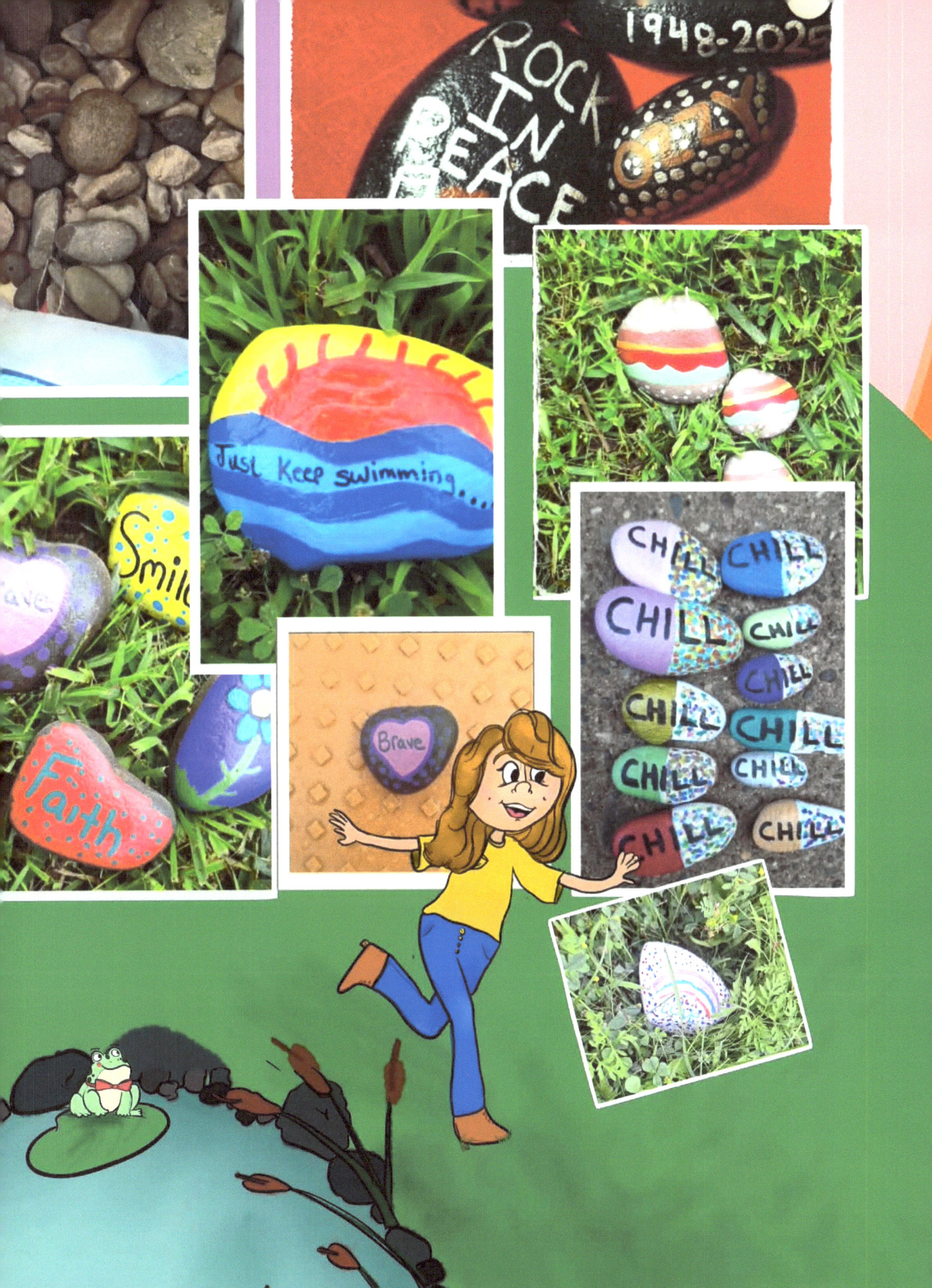
ROCK IN PEACE
1948-2025
OZZY
Just Keep swimming...
Faith
Brave
CHILL

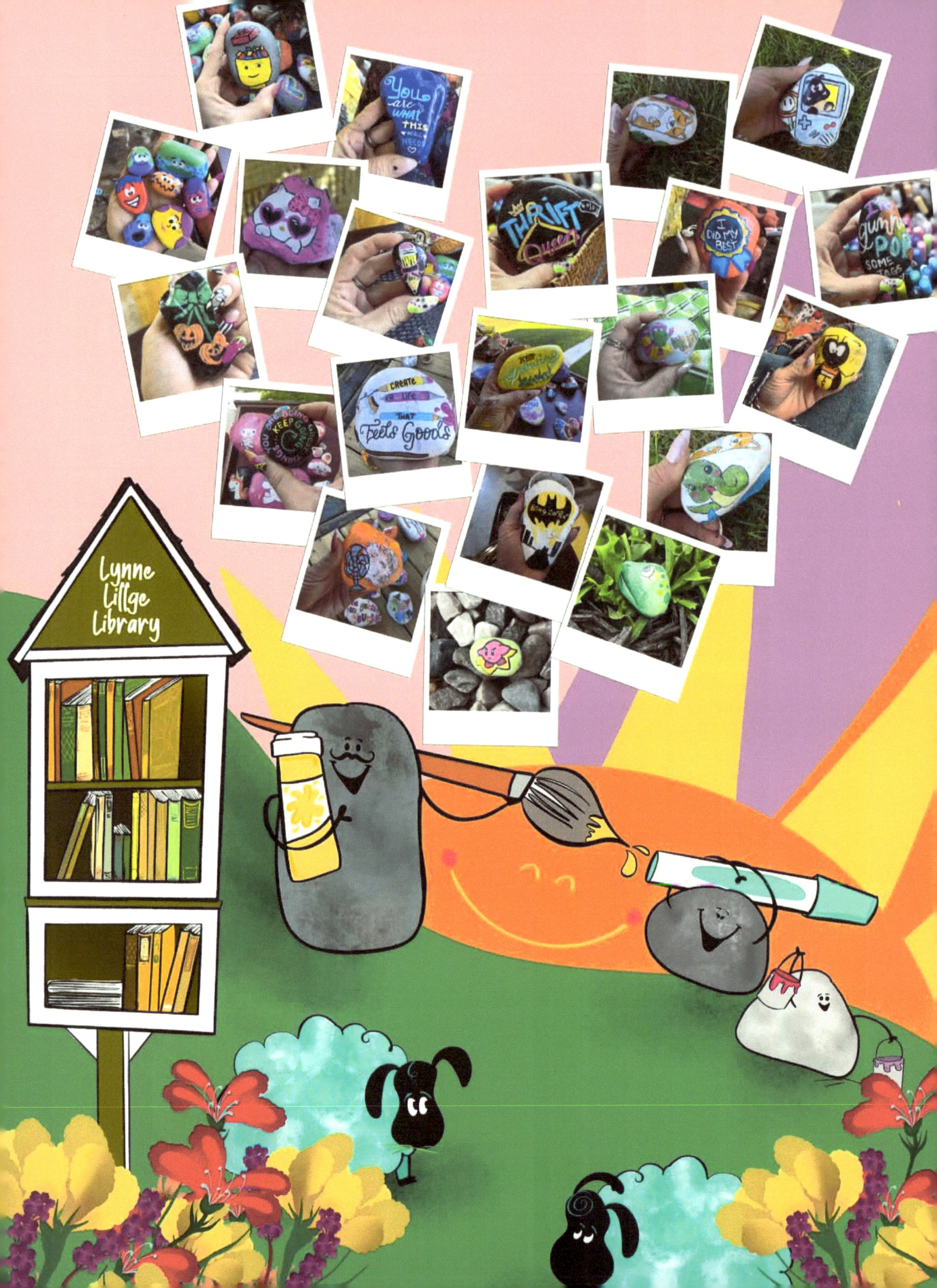
Lynne Lillge Library
THRIFT Queen
I DID MY BEST
CREATE A LIFE THAT Feels Good

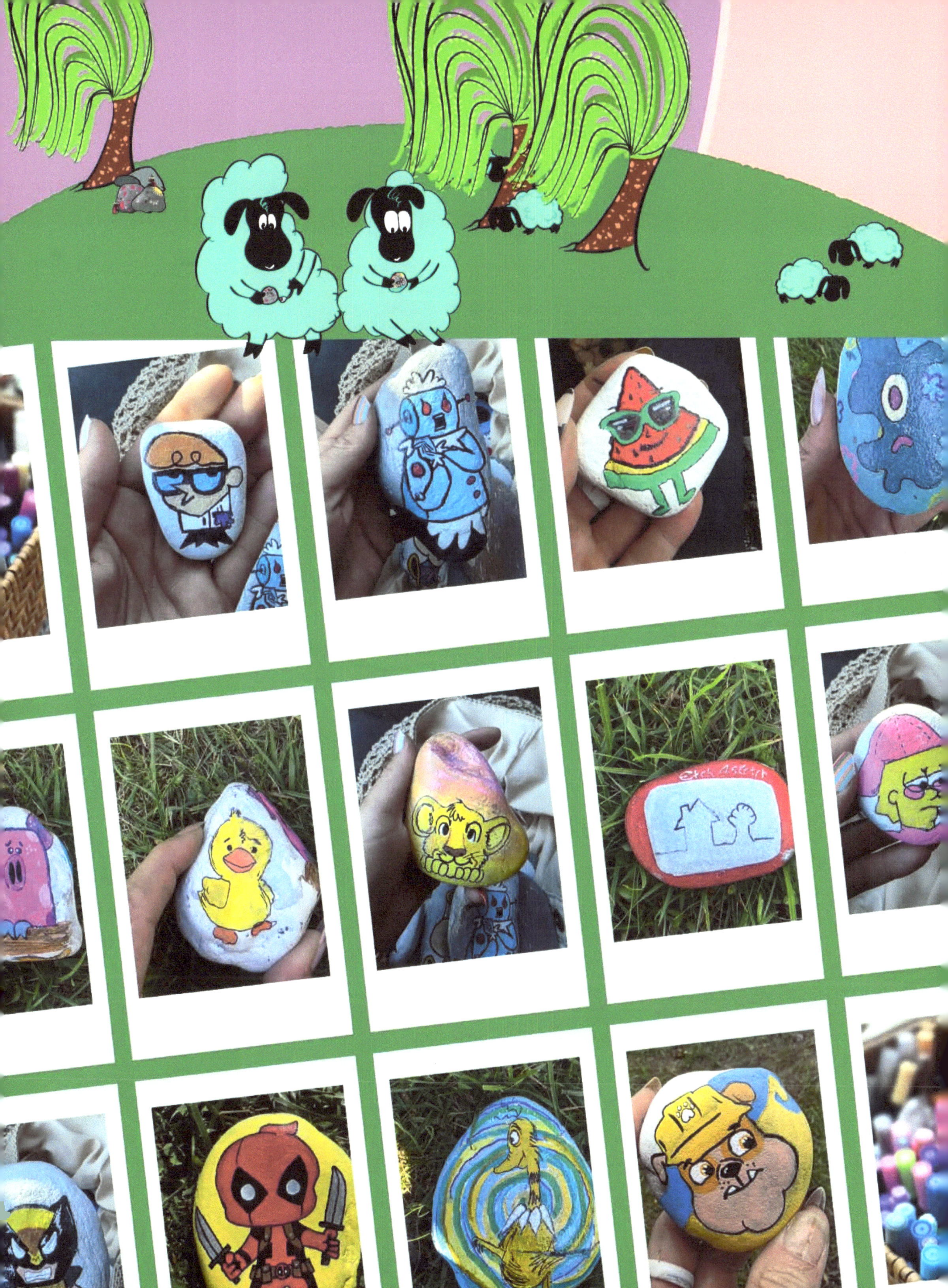

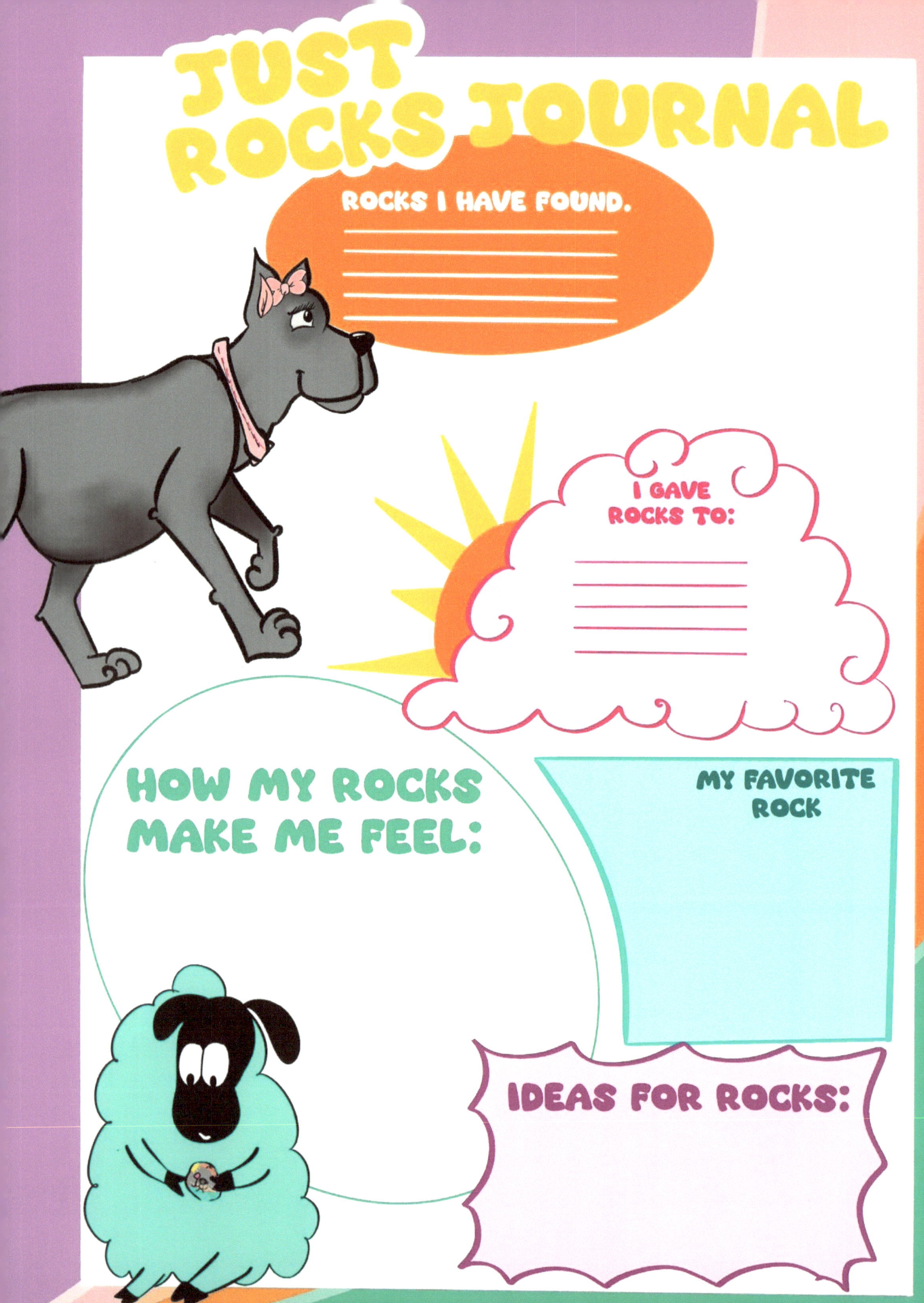
JUST ROCKS JOURNAL
ROCKS I HAVE FOUND.
I GAVE ROCKS TO:
HOW MY ROCKS MAKE ME FEEL:
MY FAVORITE ROCK
IDEAS FOR ROCKS:

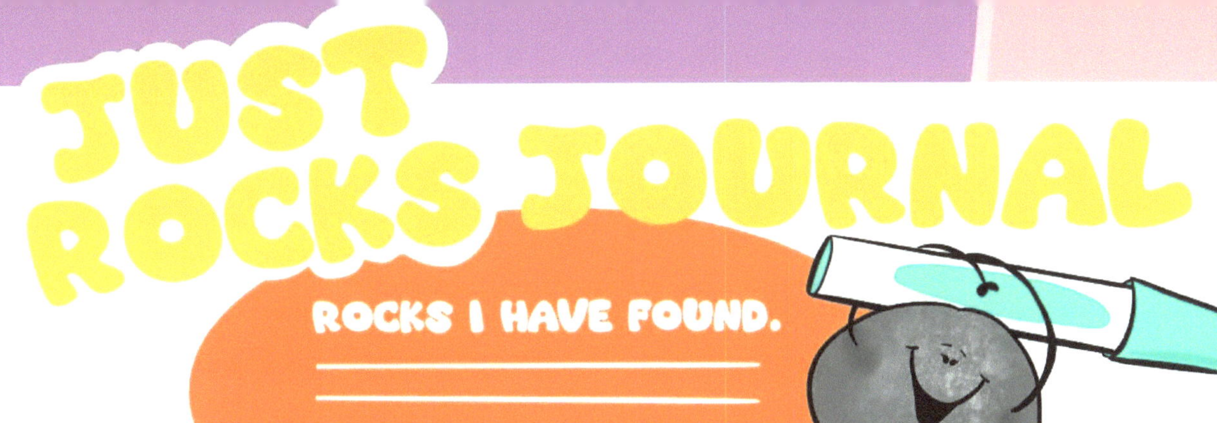

# JUST ROCKS JOURNAL

ROCKS I HAVE FOUND.

MY FAVORITE ROCK

I GAVE ROCKS TO:

## HOW MY ROCKS MAKE ME FEEL:

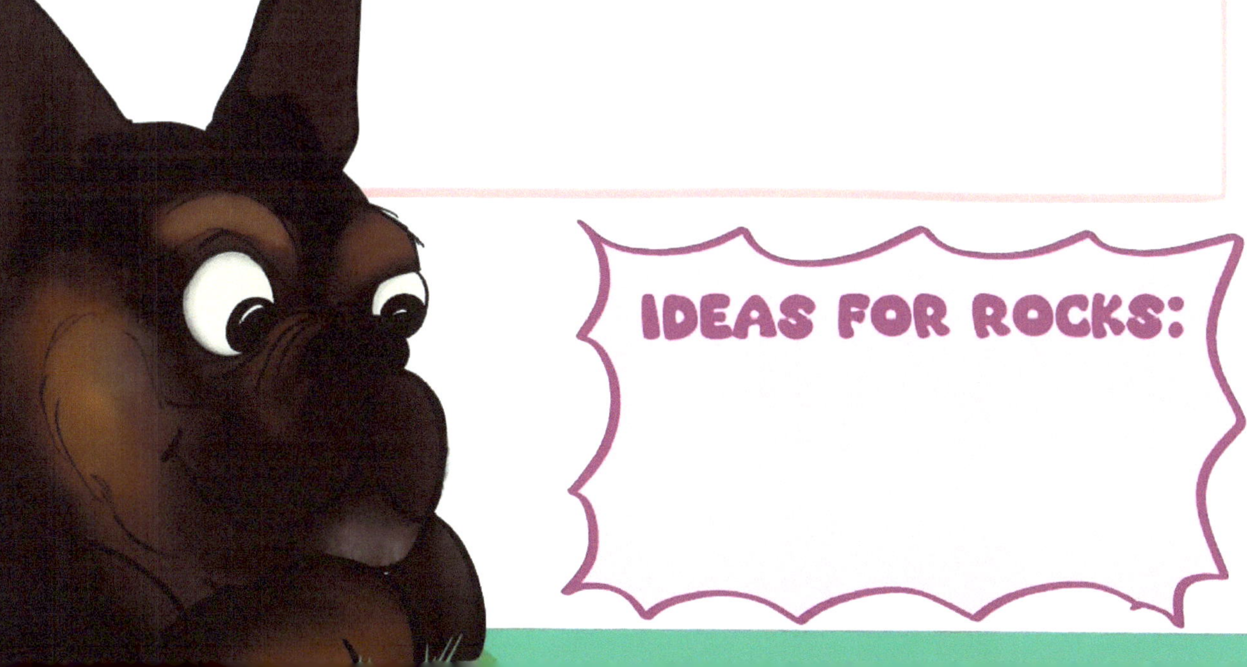

IDEAS FOR ROCKS:

# JUST ROCKS JOURNAL

ROCKS I HAVE FOUND.

MY FAVORITE ROCK

I GAVE ROCKS TO:

## HOW MY ROCKS MAKE ME FEEL:

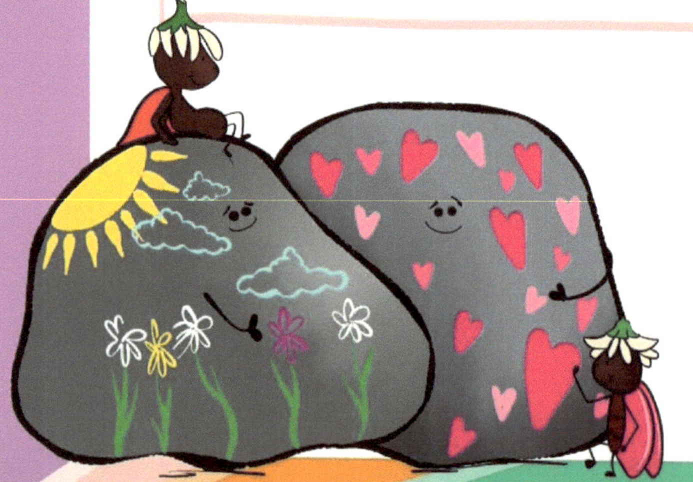

IDEAS FOR ROCKS:

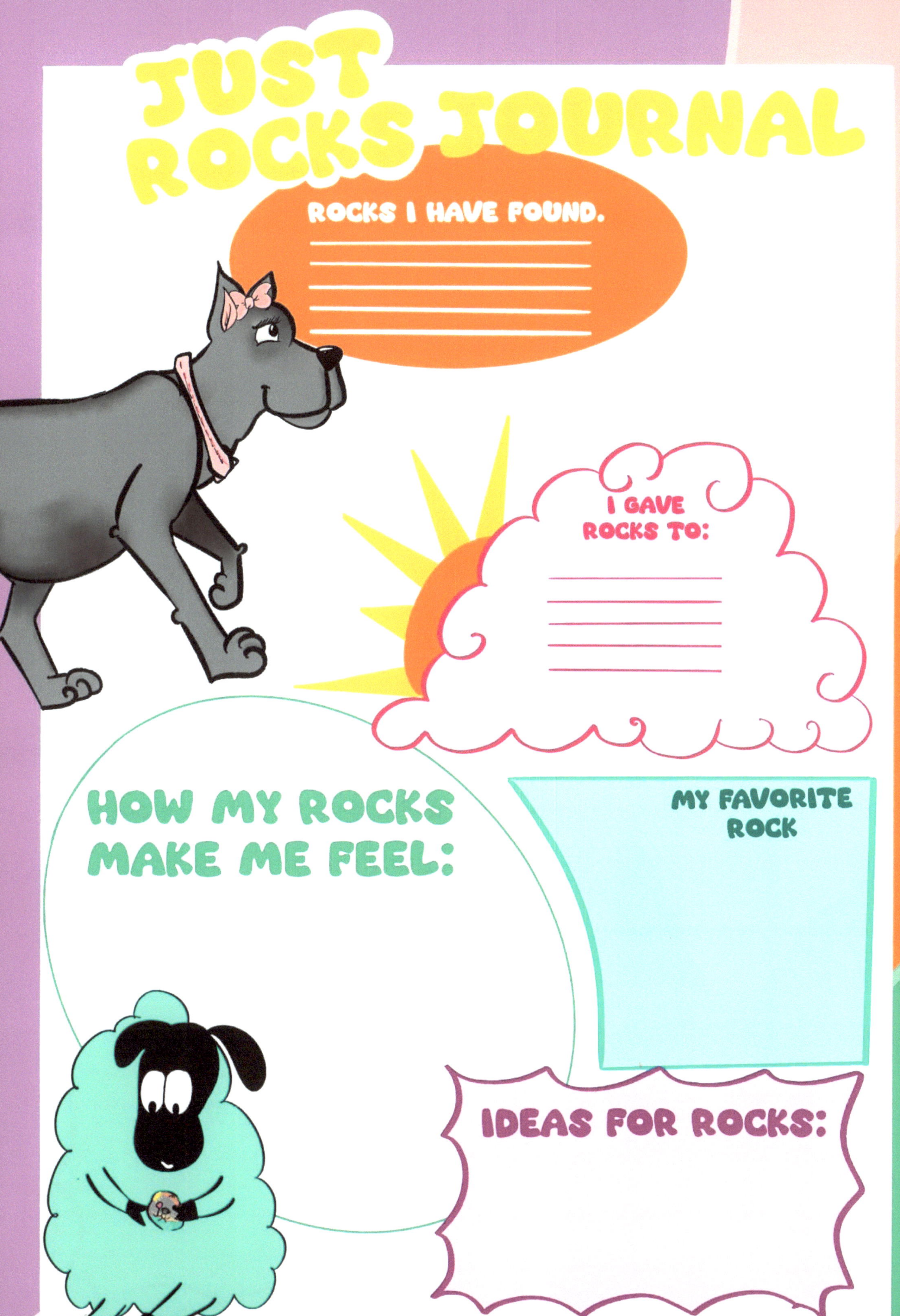
JUST ROCKS JOURNAL
ROCKS I HAVE FOUND.
I GAVE ROCKS TO:
HOW MY ROCKS MAKE ME FEEL:
MY FAVORITE ROCK
IDEAS FOR ROCKS:

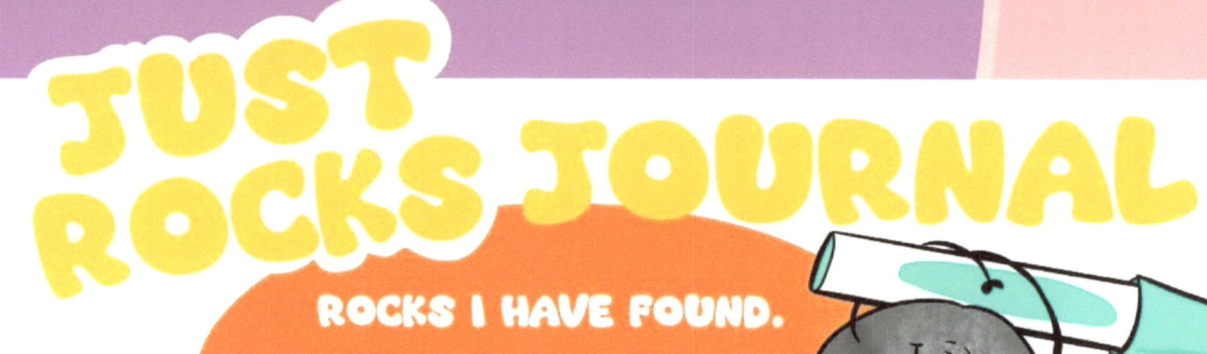


ROCKS I HAVE FOUND.

MY FAVORITE ROCK

I GAVE ROCKS TO:

HOW MY ROCKS MAKE ME FEEL:

IDEAS FOR ROCKS:

# JUST ROCKS JOURNAL

ROCKS I HAVE FOUND.

MY FAVORITE ROCK

I GAVE ROCKS TO:

HOW MY ROCKS MAKE ME FEEL:

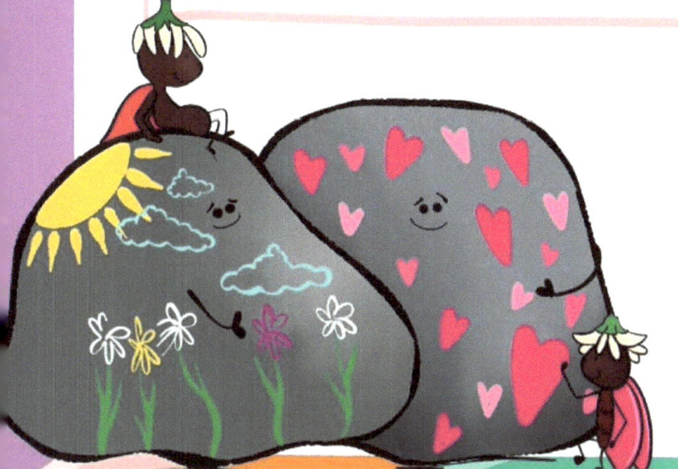

IDEAS FOR ROCKS:

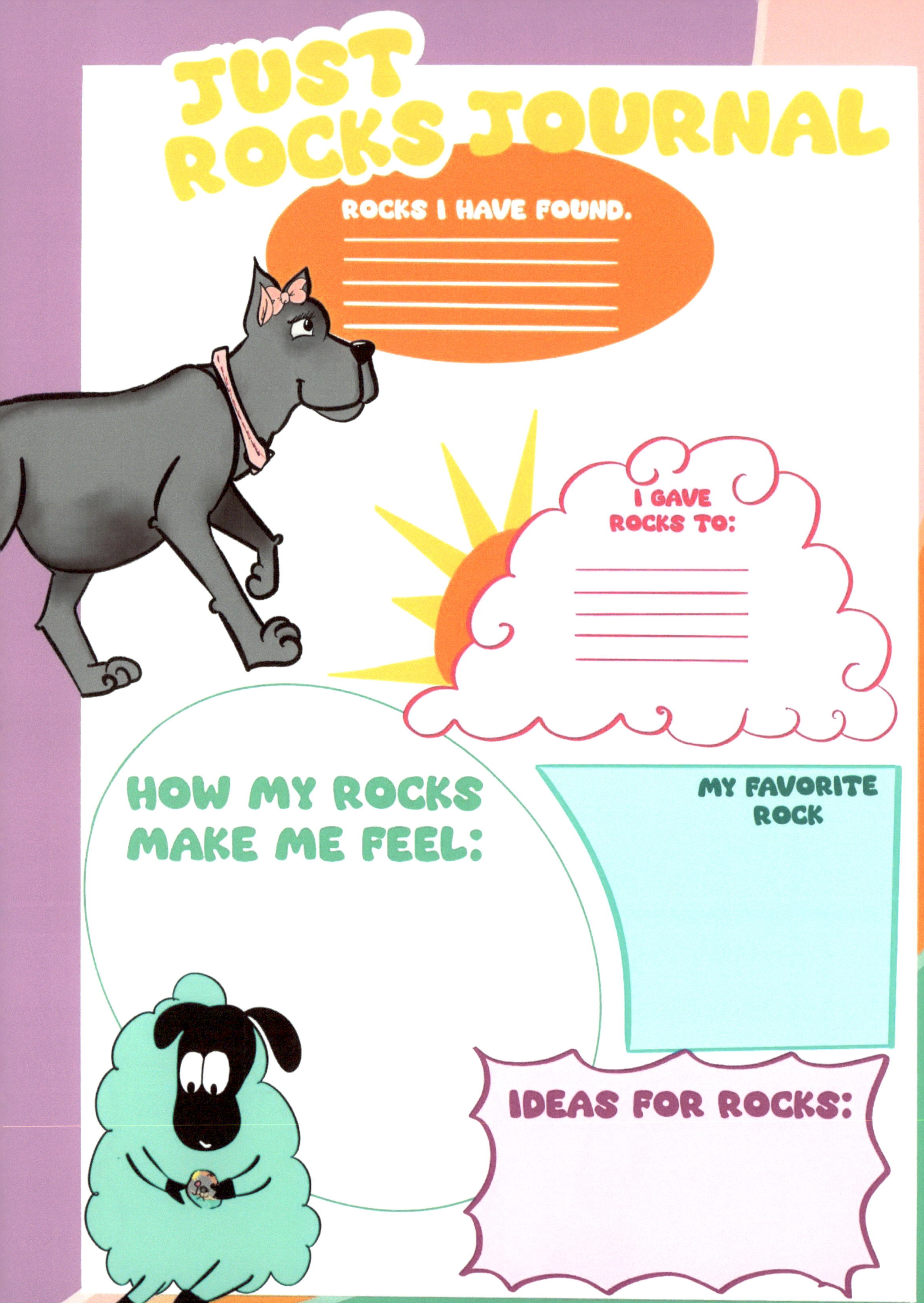
JUST ROCKS JOURNAL
ROCKS I HAVE FOUND.
I GAVE ROCKS TO:
HOW MY ROCKS MAKE ME FEEL:
MY FAVORITE ROCK
IDEAS FOR ROCKS:

# JUST ROCKS JOURNAL

ROCKS I HAVE FOUND.

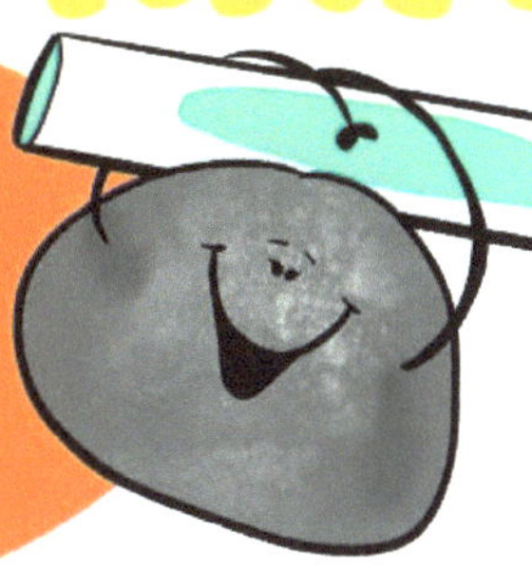

MY FAVORITE ROCK

I GAVE ROCKS TO:

## HOW MY ROCKS MAKE ME FEEL:

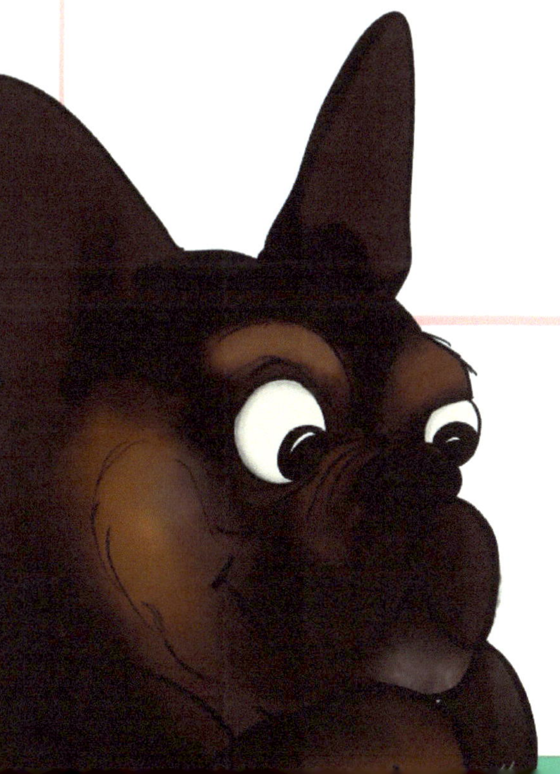

IDEAS FOR ROCKS:

# JUST ROCKS JOURNAL

ROCKS I HAVE FOUND.

MY FAVORITE ROCK

I GAVE ROCKS TO:

HOW MY ROCKS MAKE ME FEEL:

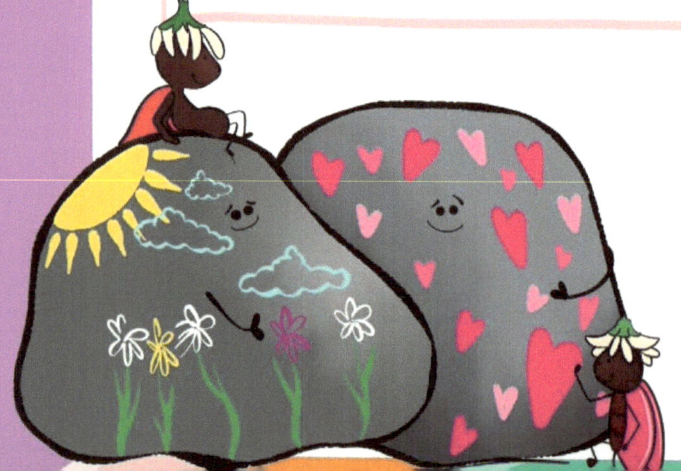

IDEAS FOR ROCKS:

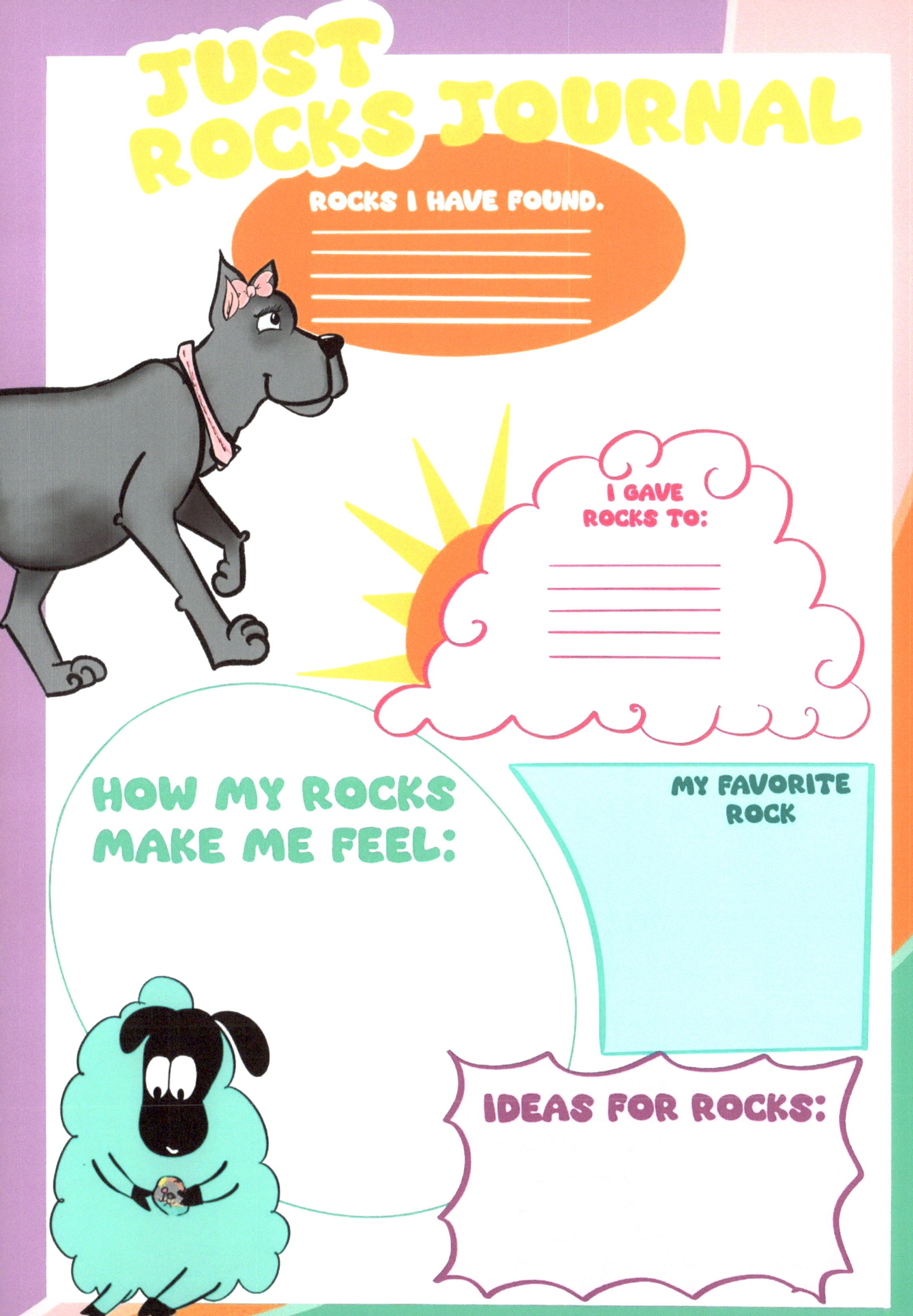
JUST ROCKS JOURNAL
ROCKS I HAVE FOUND.
I GAVE ROCKS TO:
HOW MY ROCKS MAKE ME FEEL:
MY FAVORITE ROCK
IDEAS FOR ROCKS:

# IDEAS FOR HIDING JUST *painted* ROCKS

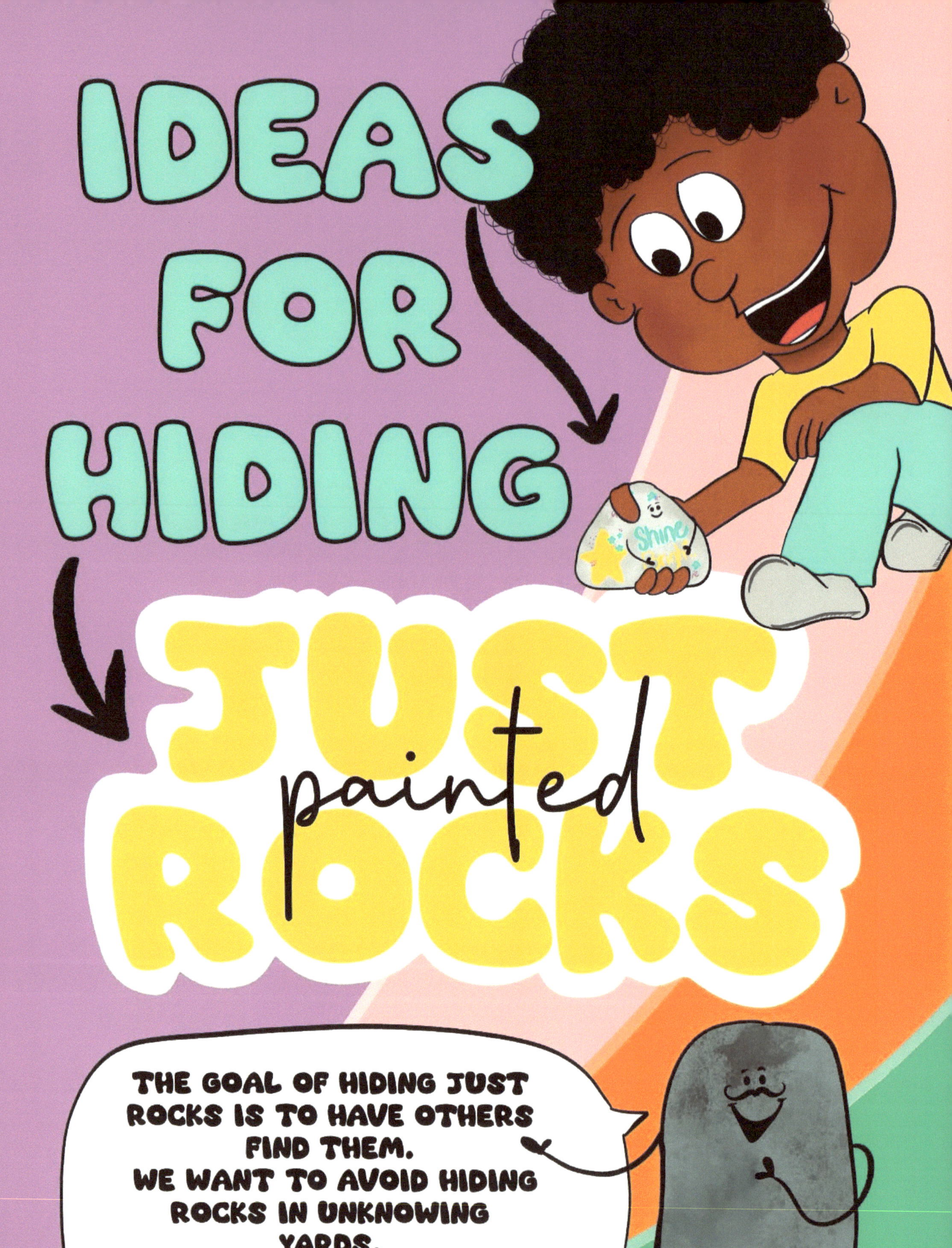

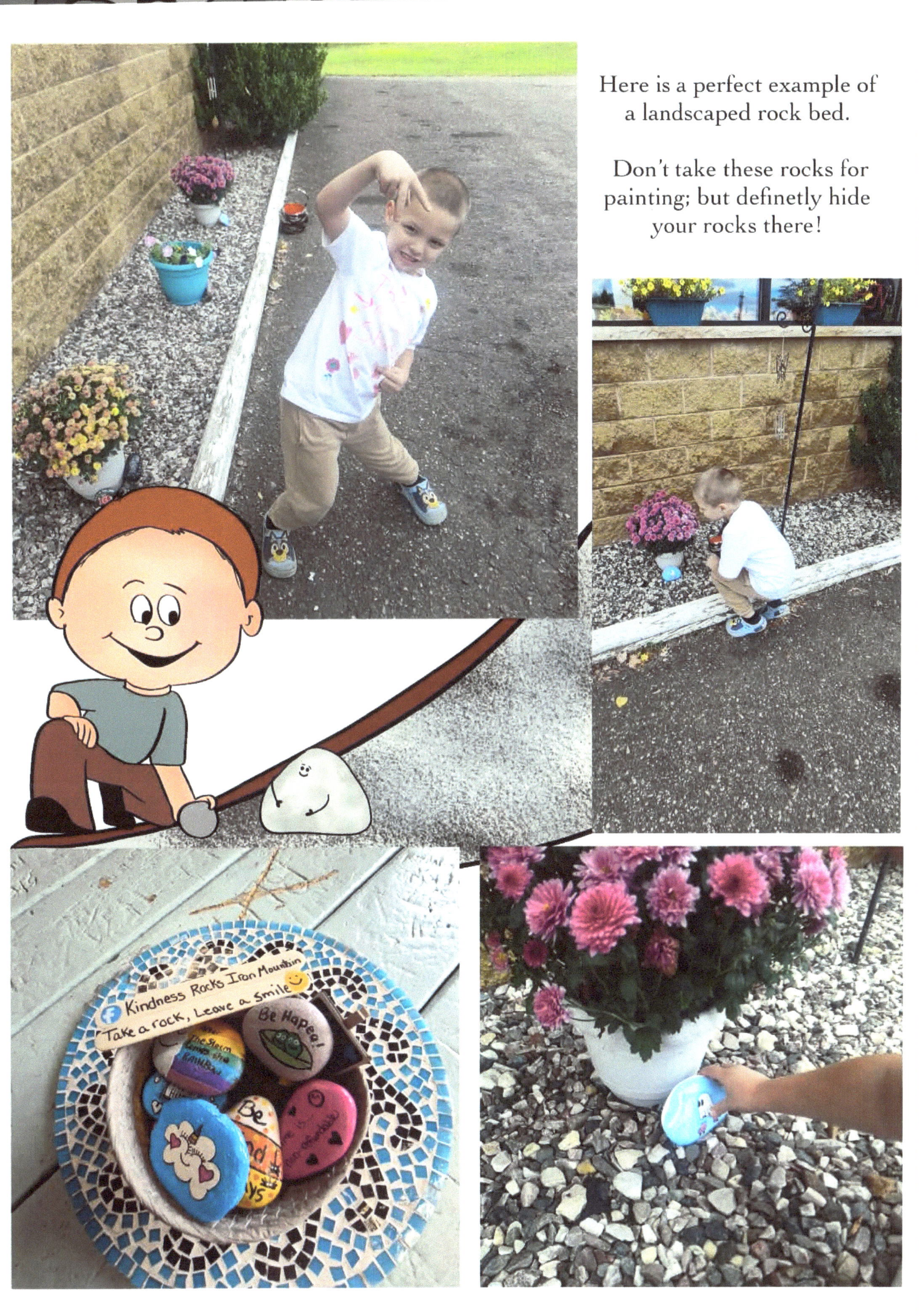
Here is a perfect example of
a landscaped rock bed.
Don't take these rocks for
painting; but definetly hide
your rocks there!
Kindness Rocks Iron Mountain
Take a rock, Leave a smile
Be Hapea!

# HOSPITALS ARE WELCOME HOMES

Medical facilities of all types are great hiding spots for your rocks. A lot of them have rocks as landscaping or designated sidewalks.

If you are worried about your rocks rolling away, consider making a rock basket and ask to place it at the check in.

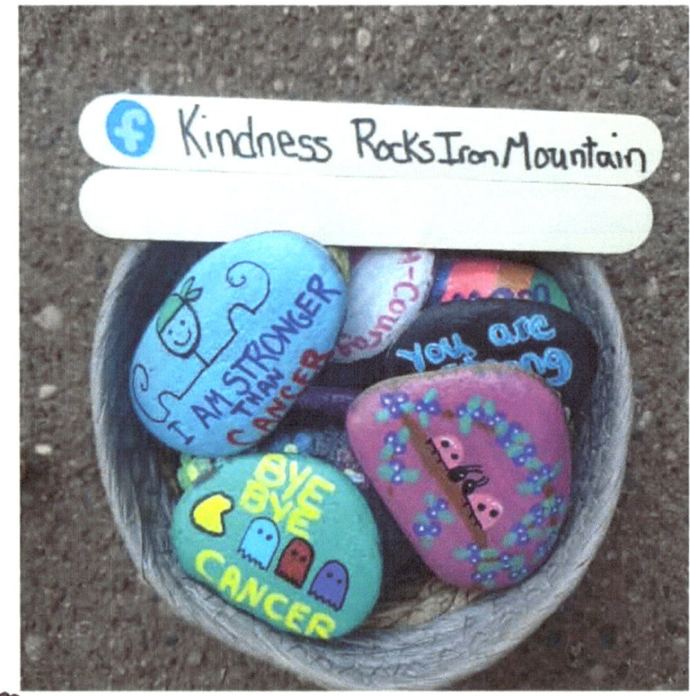


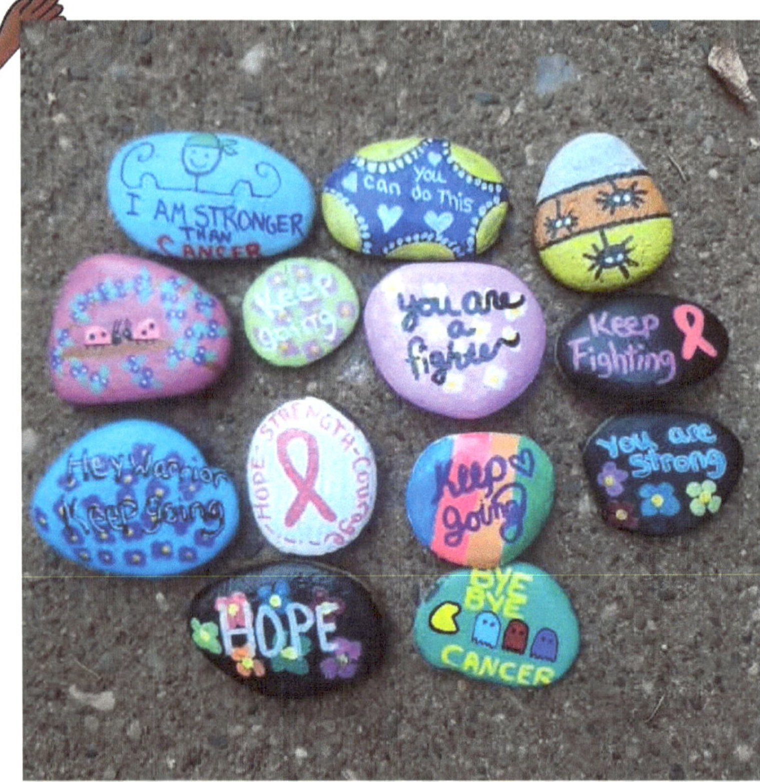

# BUS DRIVERS MAKE GREAT INSPIRATION!

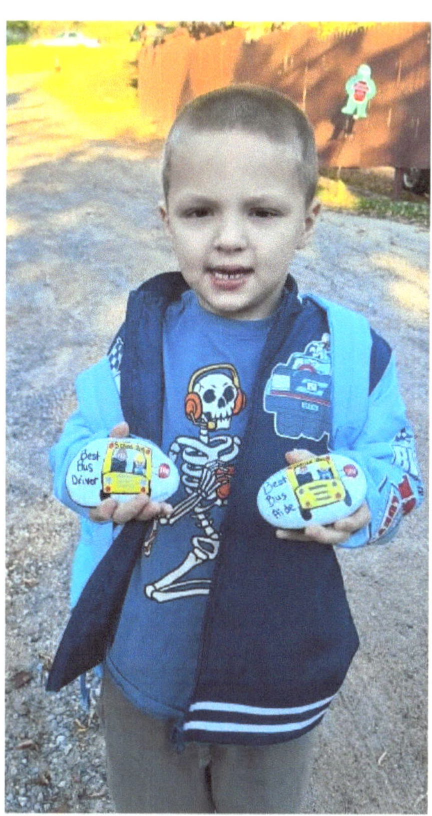


🌞 Started the day off spreading a little extra kindness! 💕 My son wanted to surprise his bus driver and bus aide — two people he absolutely adores — with some special rocks this morning. 🚌💖 They loved them so much!! Mission accomplished! 🎨💪

Not gonna lie… these were trickier to make than I expected 😅 but I gave it my best shot — and that's what it's all about! 🥰💕 Kindness, effort, and heart.

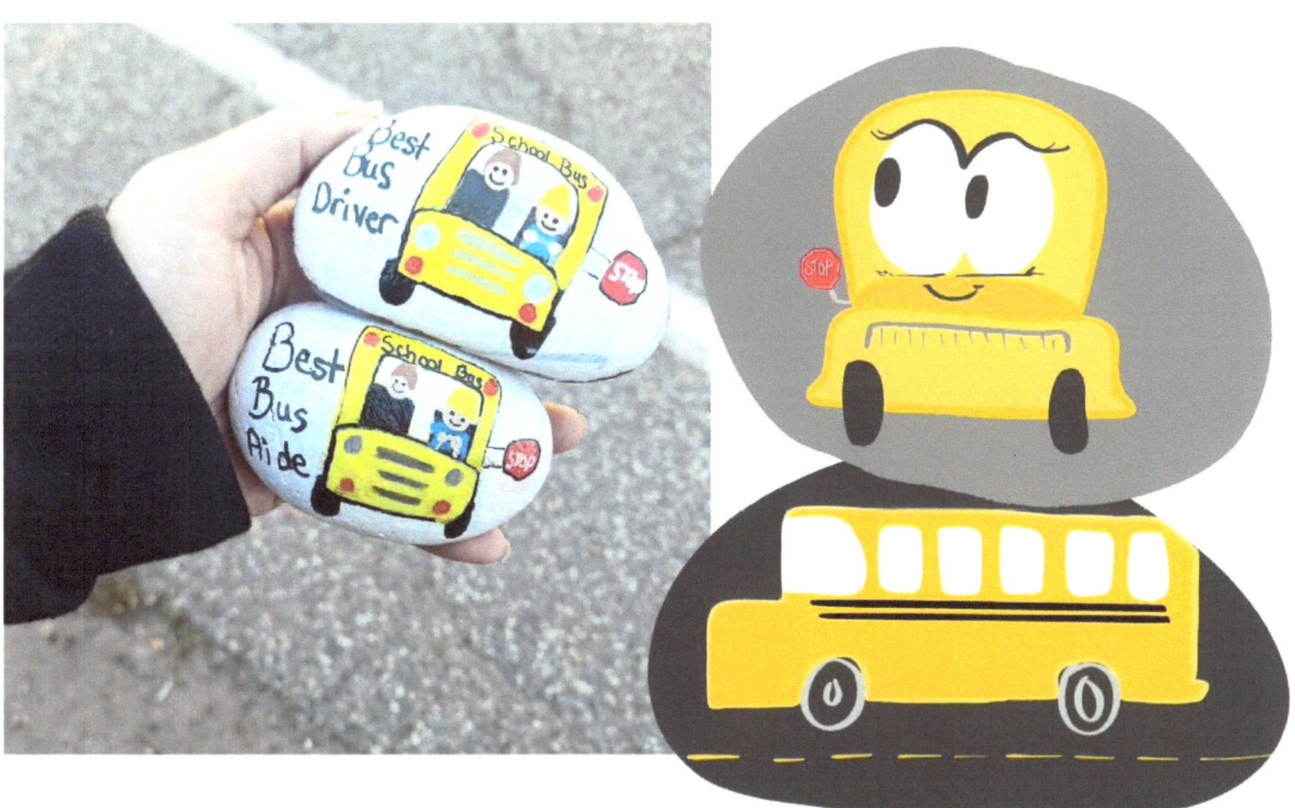

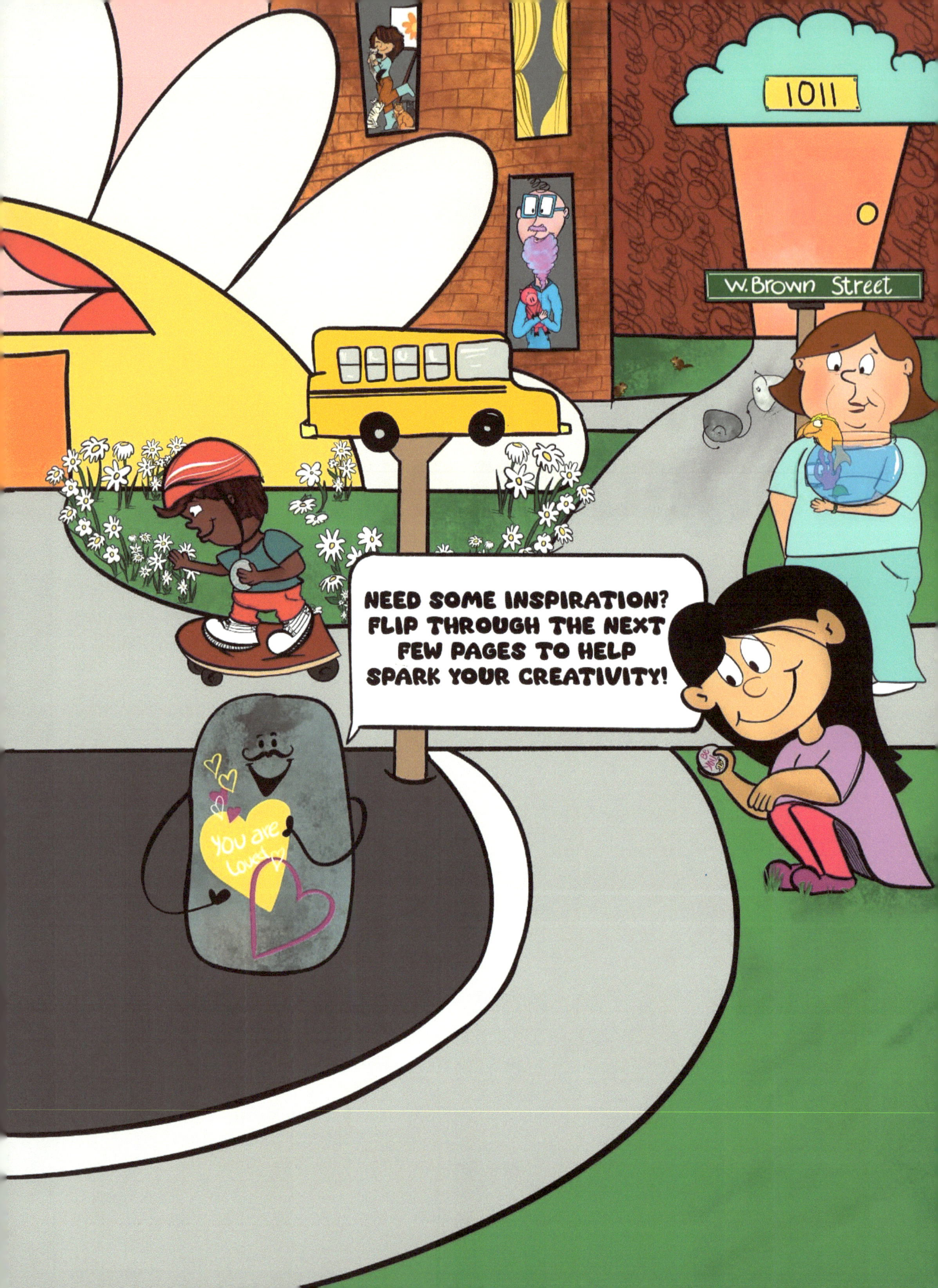
1011
W. Brown Street
NEED SOME INSPIRATION? FLIP THROUGH THE NEXT FEW PAGES TO HELP SPARK YOUR CREATIVITY!
you are Loved

# ANIMAL ROCKS!

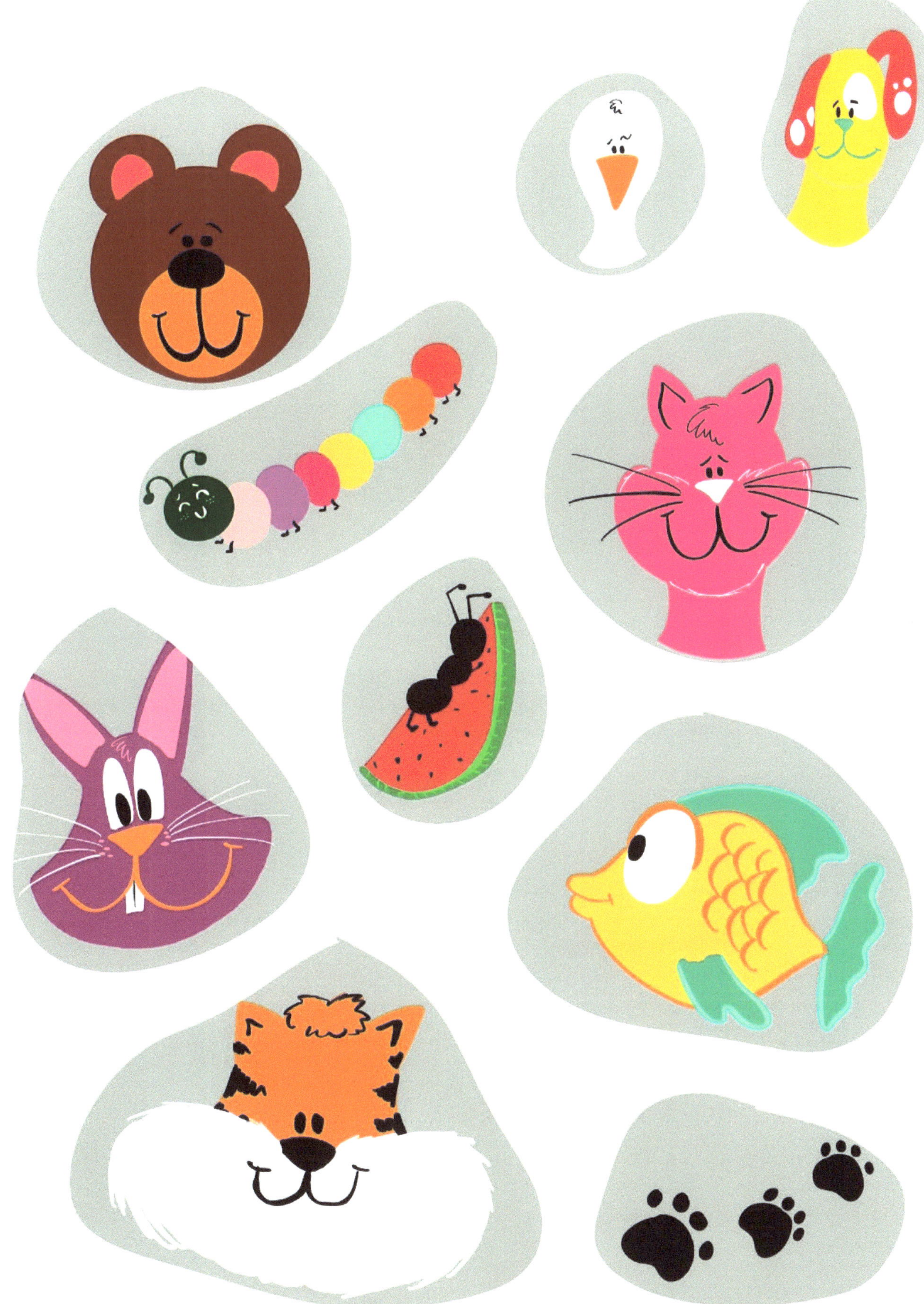

# FLORAL FRIENDS!

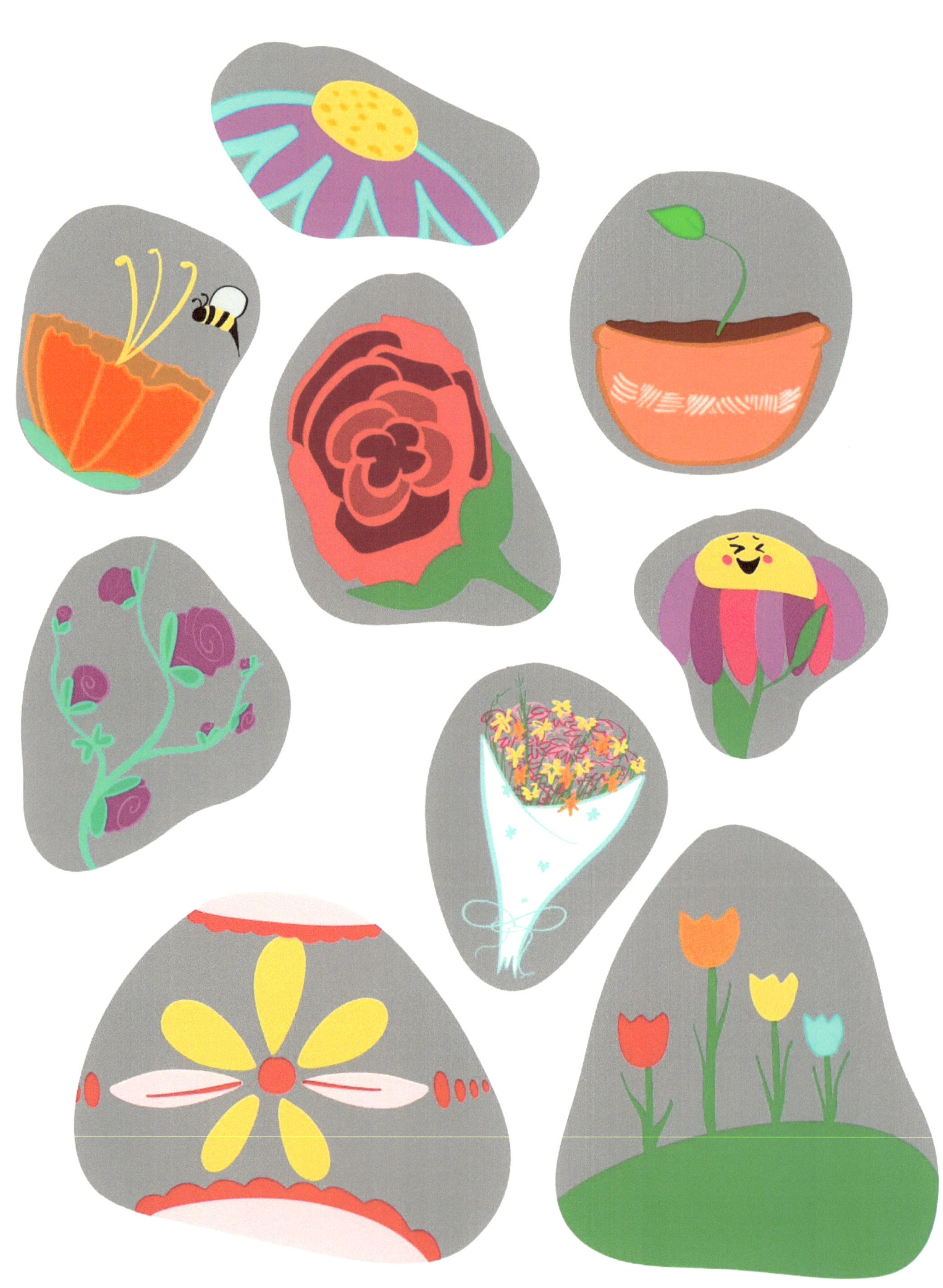

# FROZEN FRIENDS!

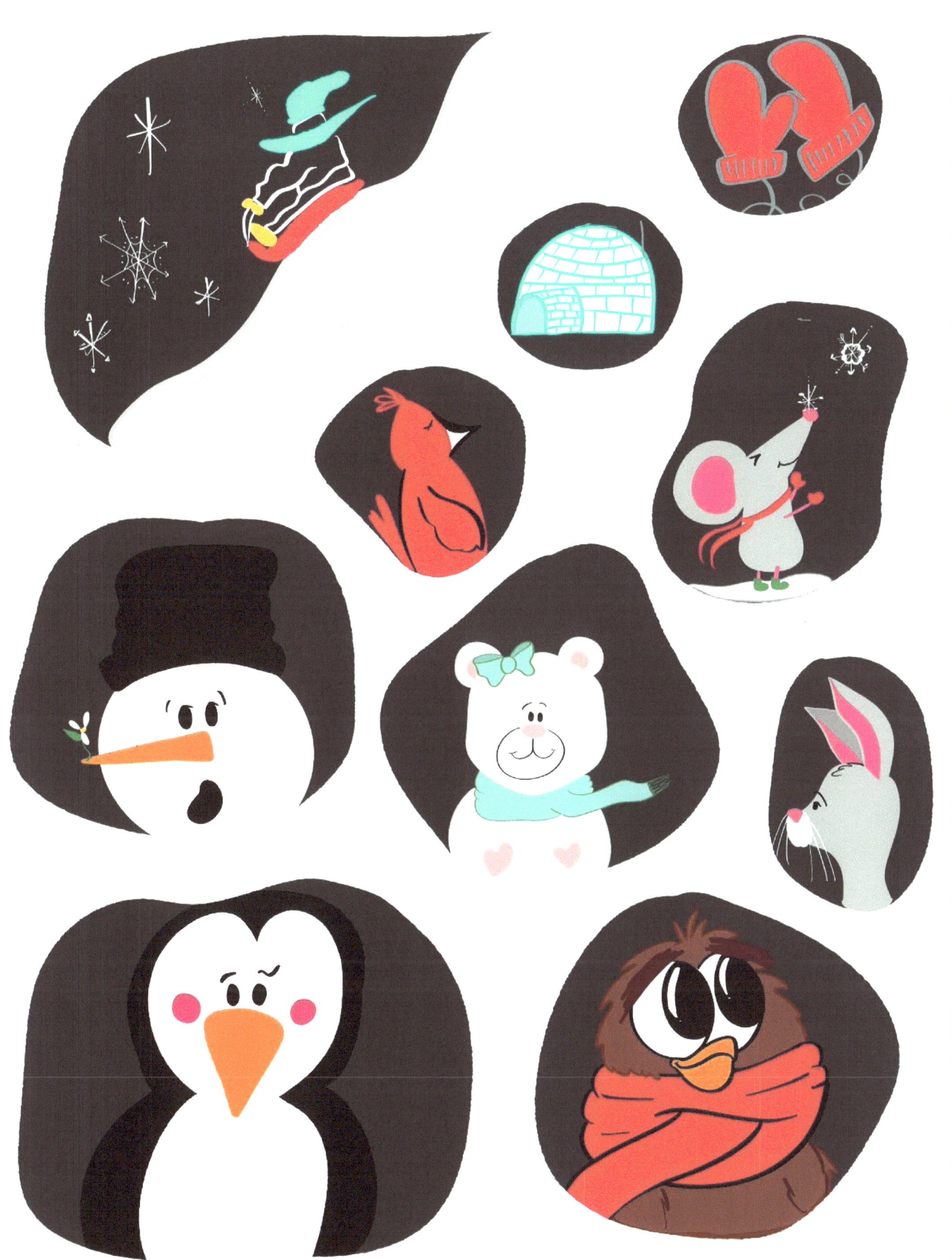

# SLEEPOVER

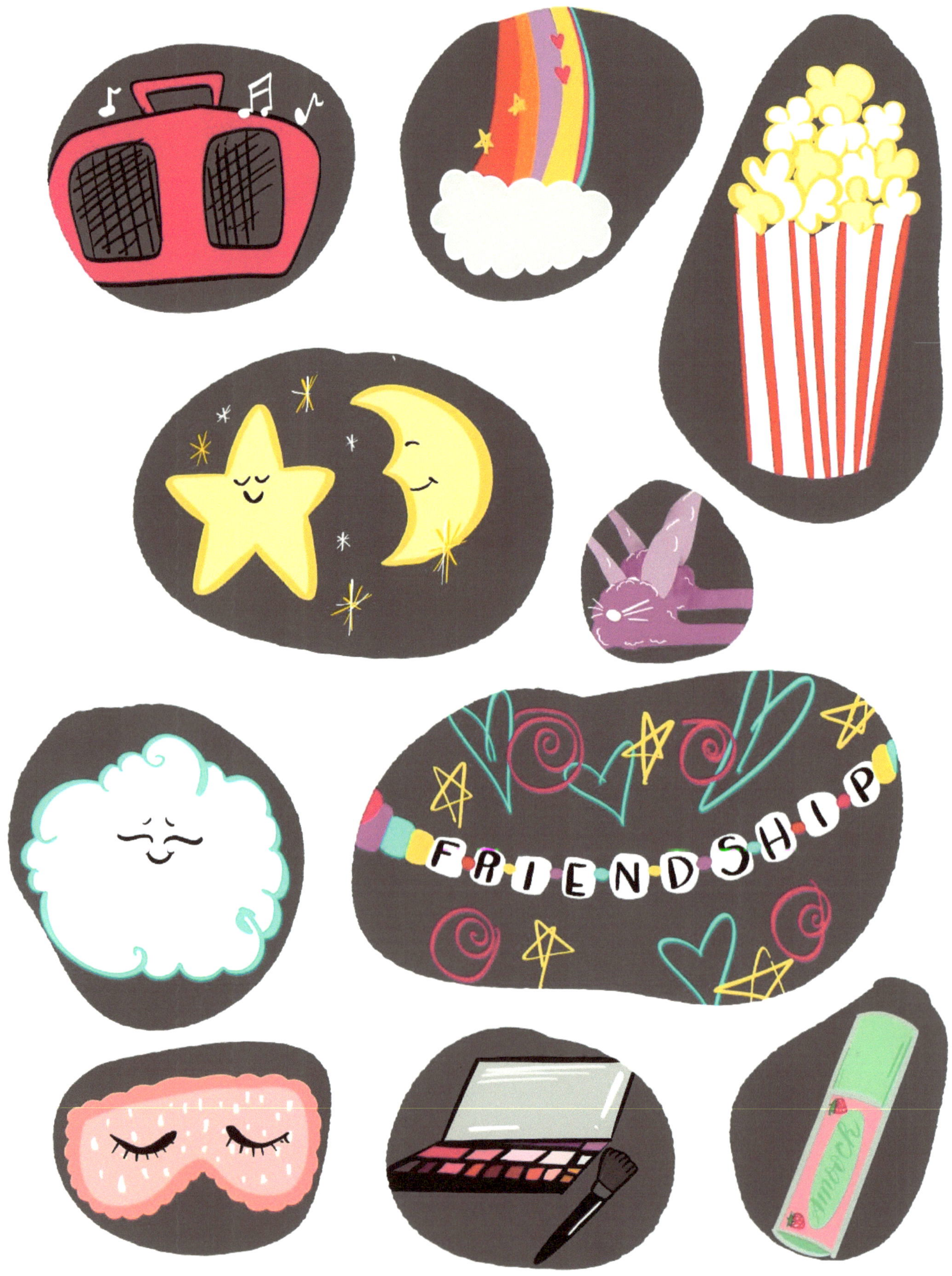

# WITH WHEELS

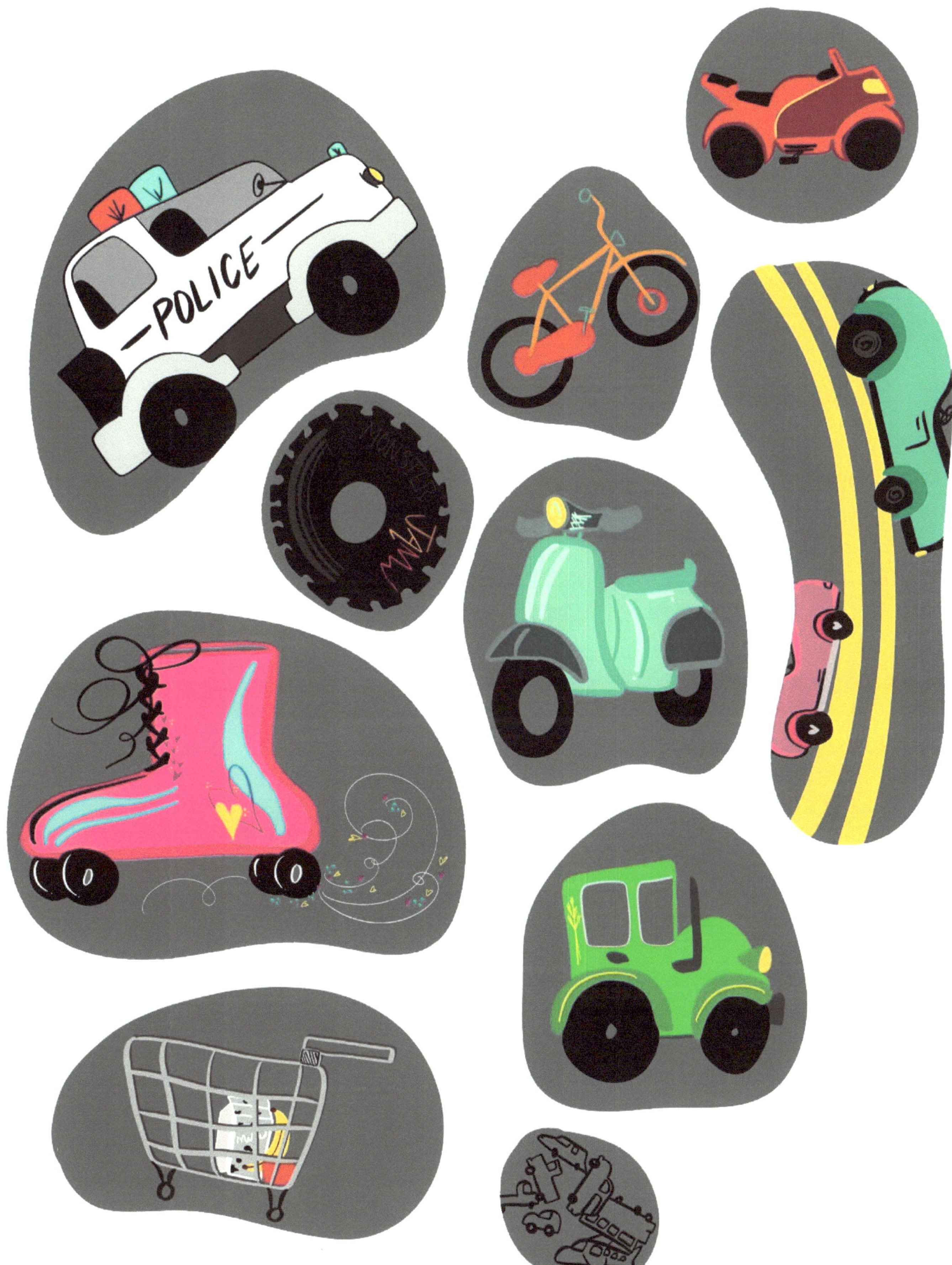

# TRAVEL

Ticket

$64

POST MARKED

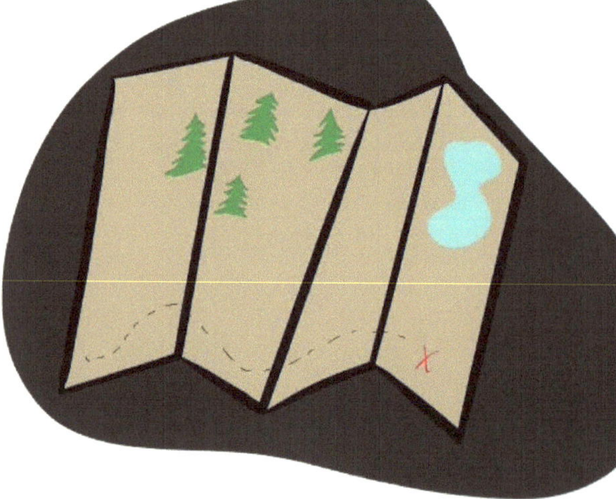

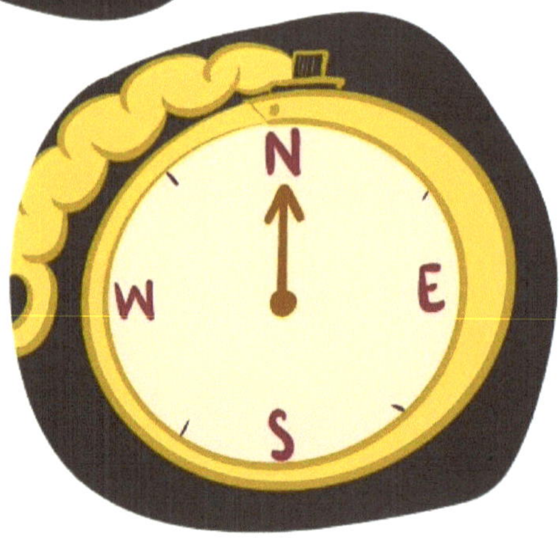

# OCEAN LIFE

# ON THE FARM

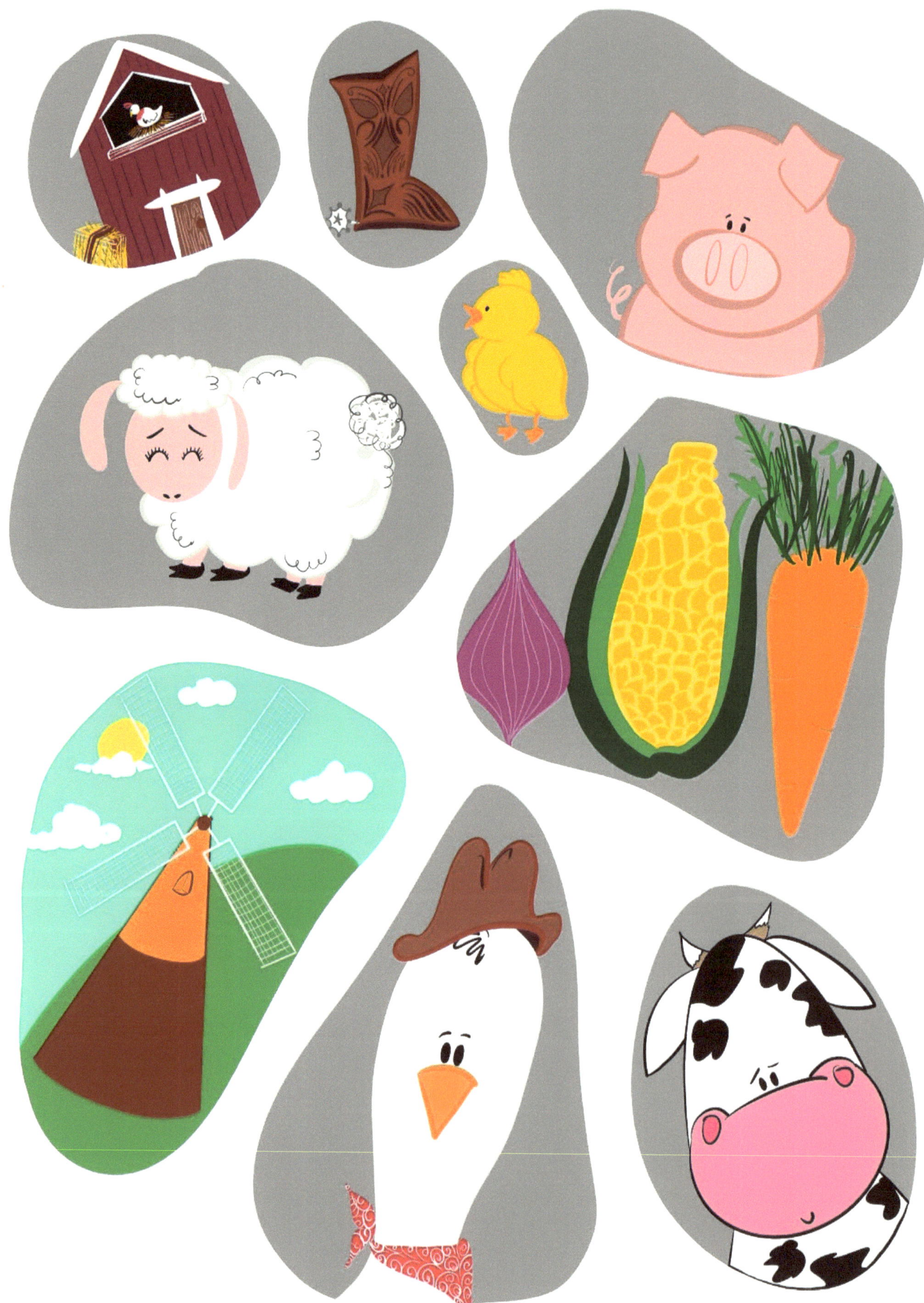

# OUTER SPACE

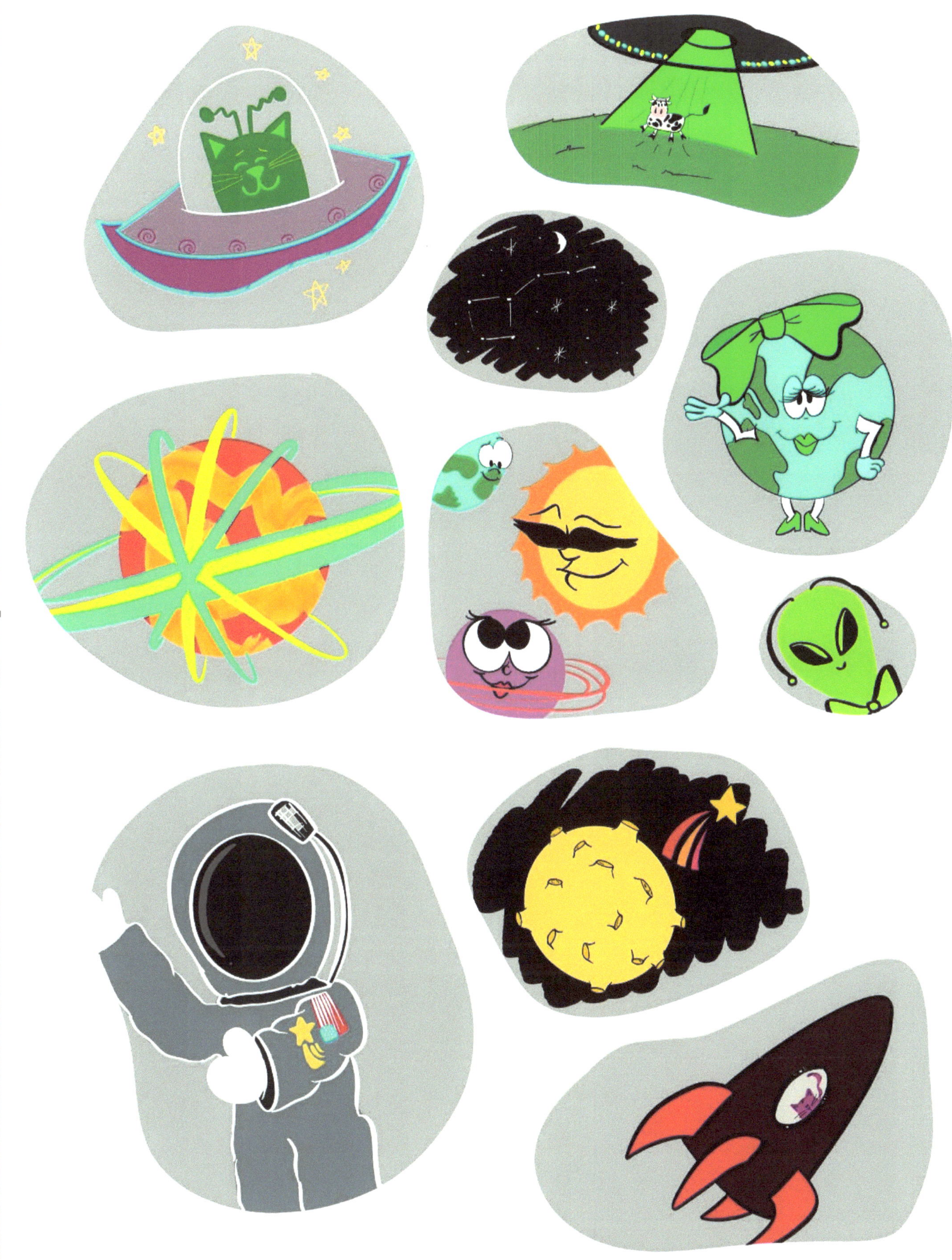

# JUST ROCKS
## Mud Kitchen

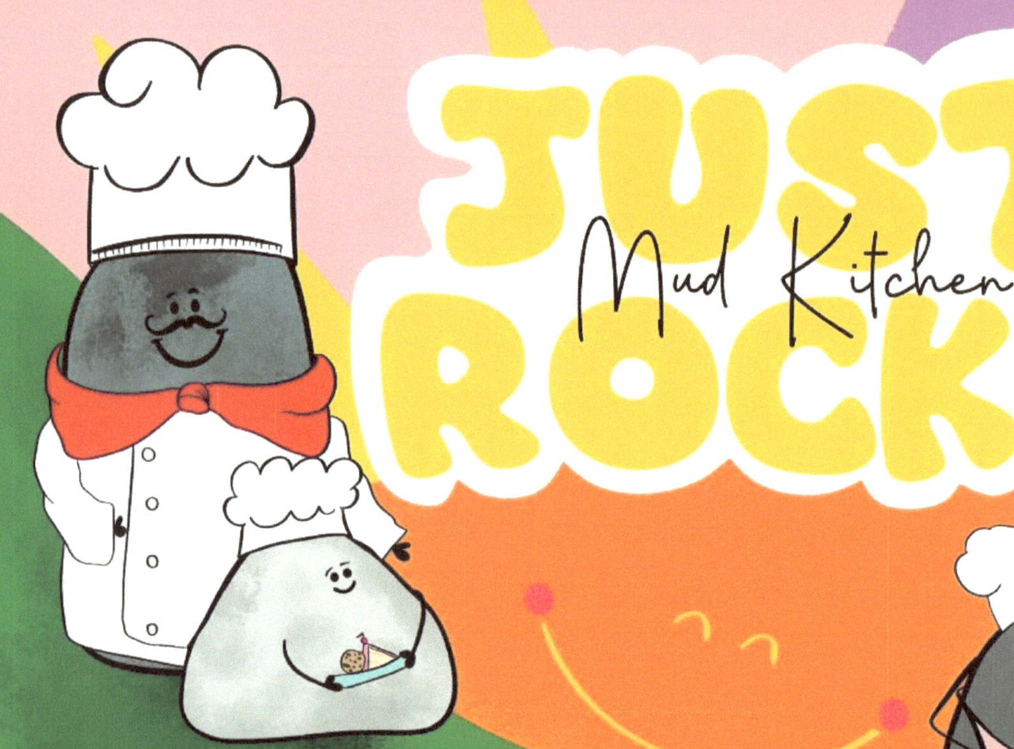

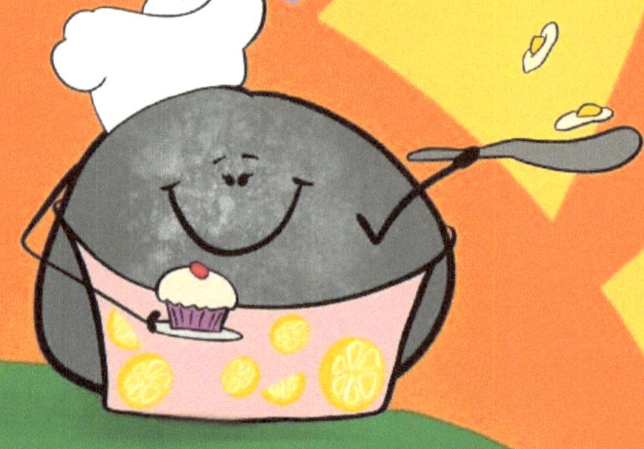

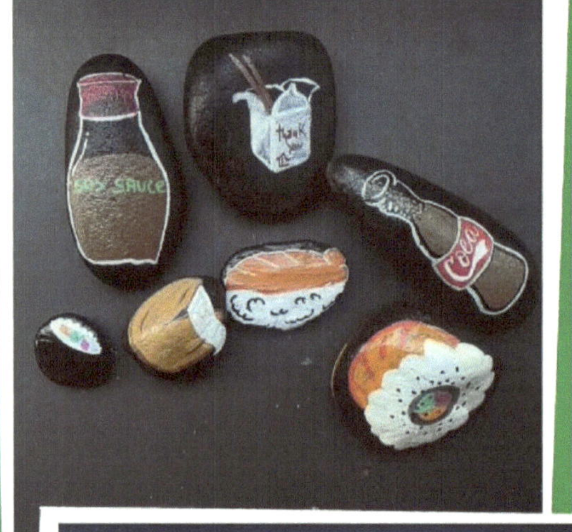


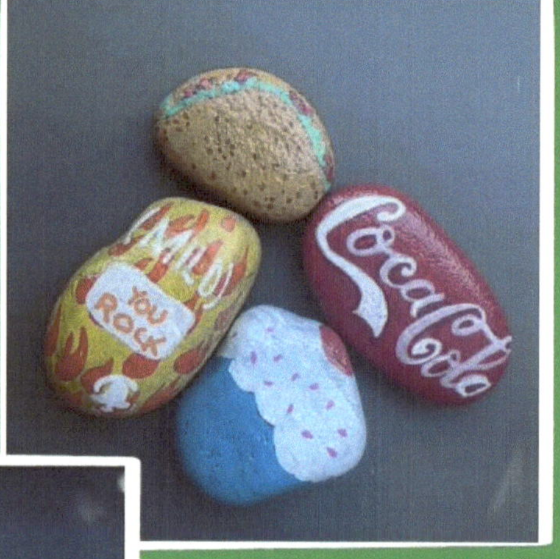


ROCKS MAKE A GREAT ADDITION TO ANY OUTDOOR KITCHEN ! MAKE UTENSILS, INGREDIENTS, AND COMPLETE DISHES !

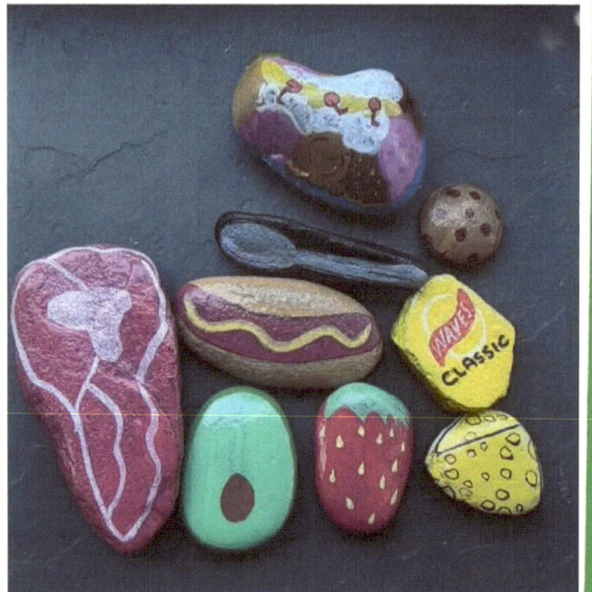


TO HELP GET THE IDEAS FLOWING TRY TO THINK OF CATEGORIES SUCH AS :

BAKERY

DESSERTS

MAIN COURSES

FOOD IN THE FREEZER SECTION

POULTRY

THANKSGIVING FEAST

BIRTHDAY PARTY FOOD

SLEEPOVER SNACK SNACKS

# BAKERY ROCKS!

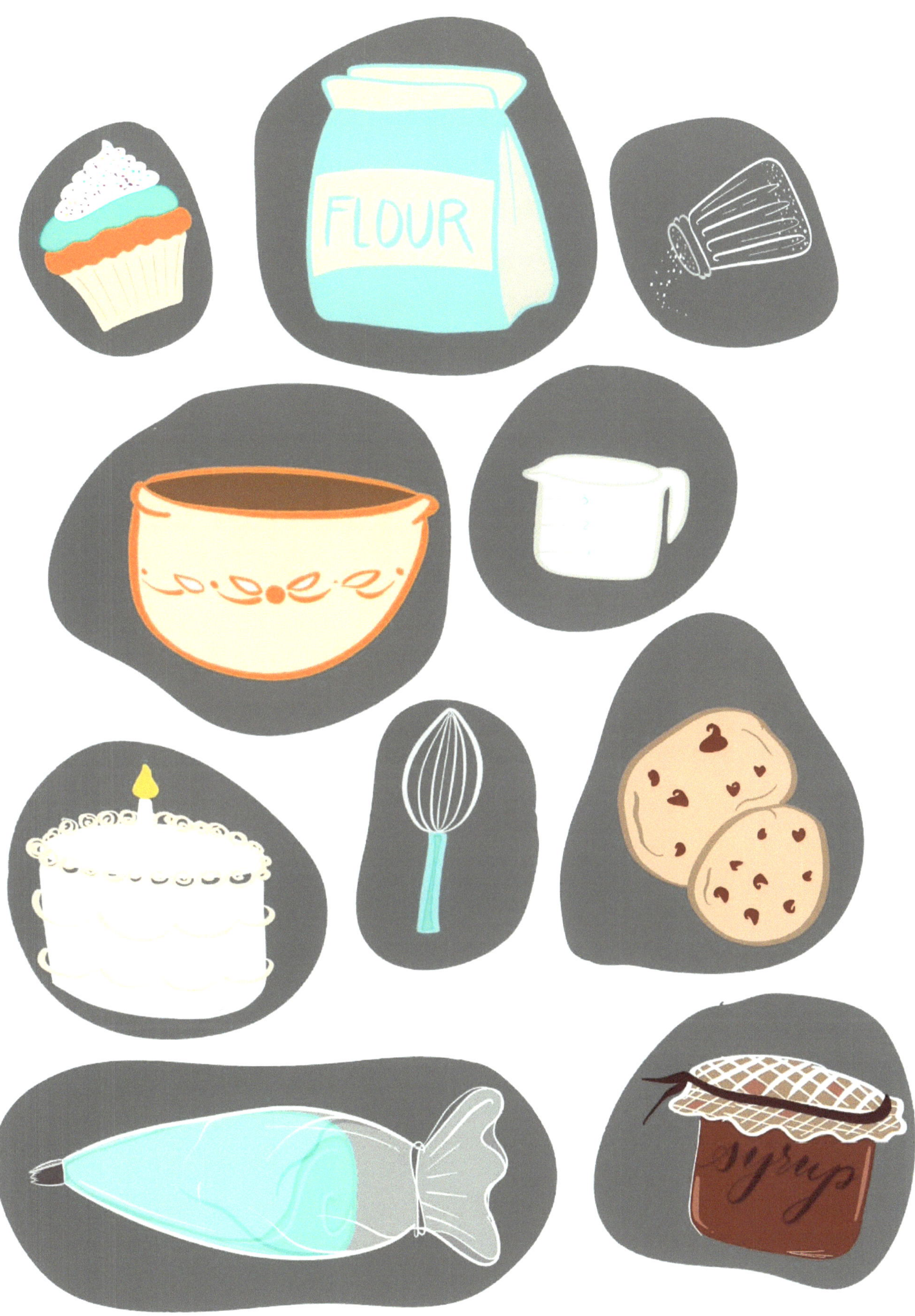

# LUNCH MENU

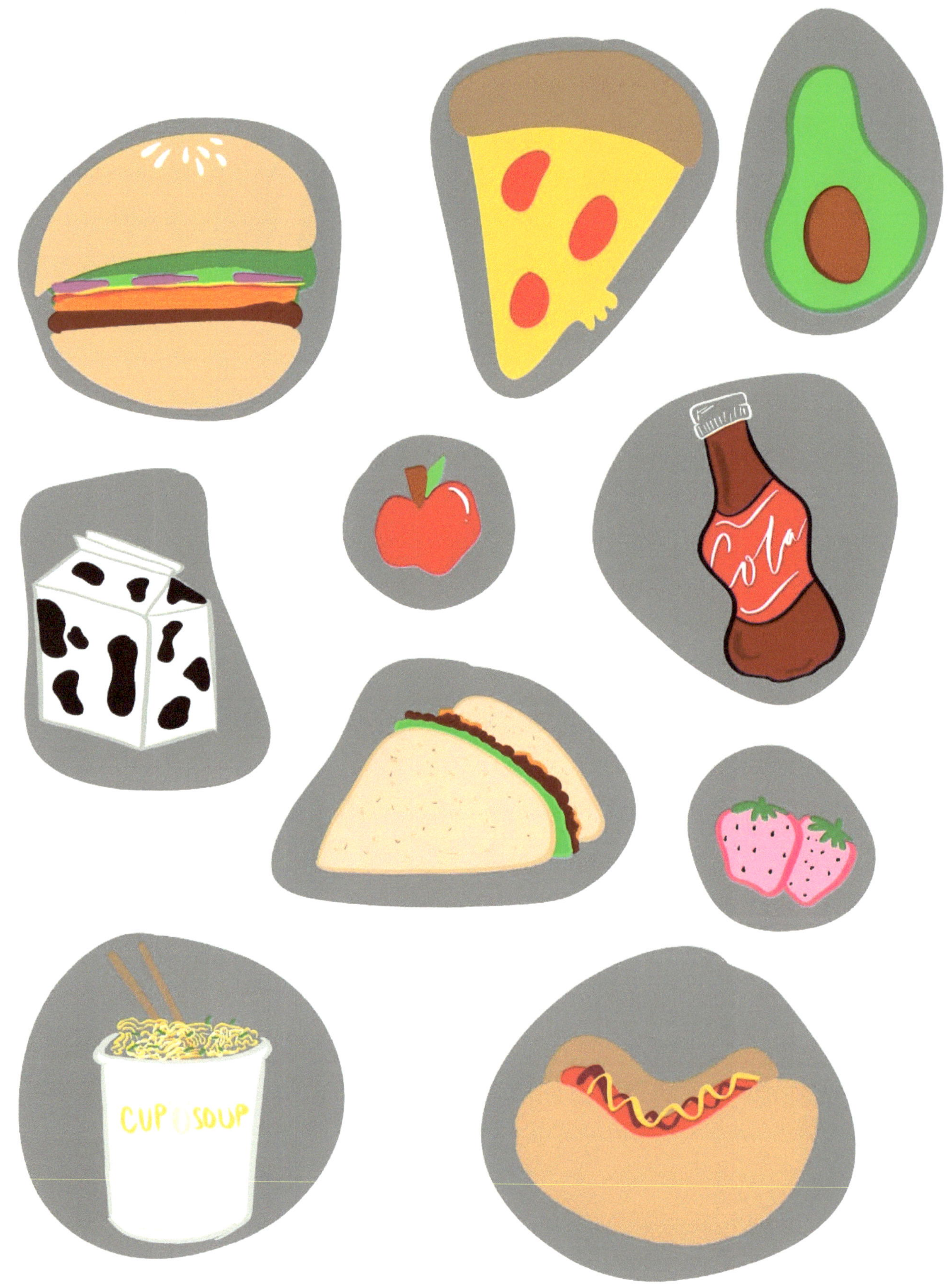

# CANDY TREATS!

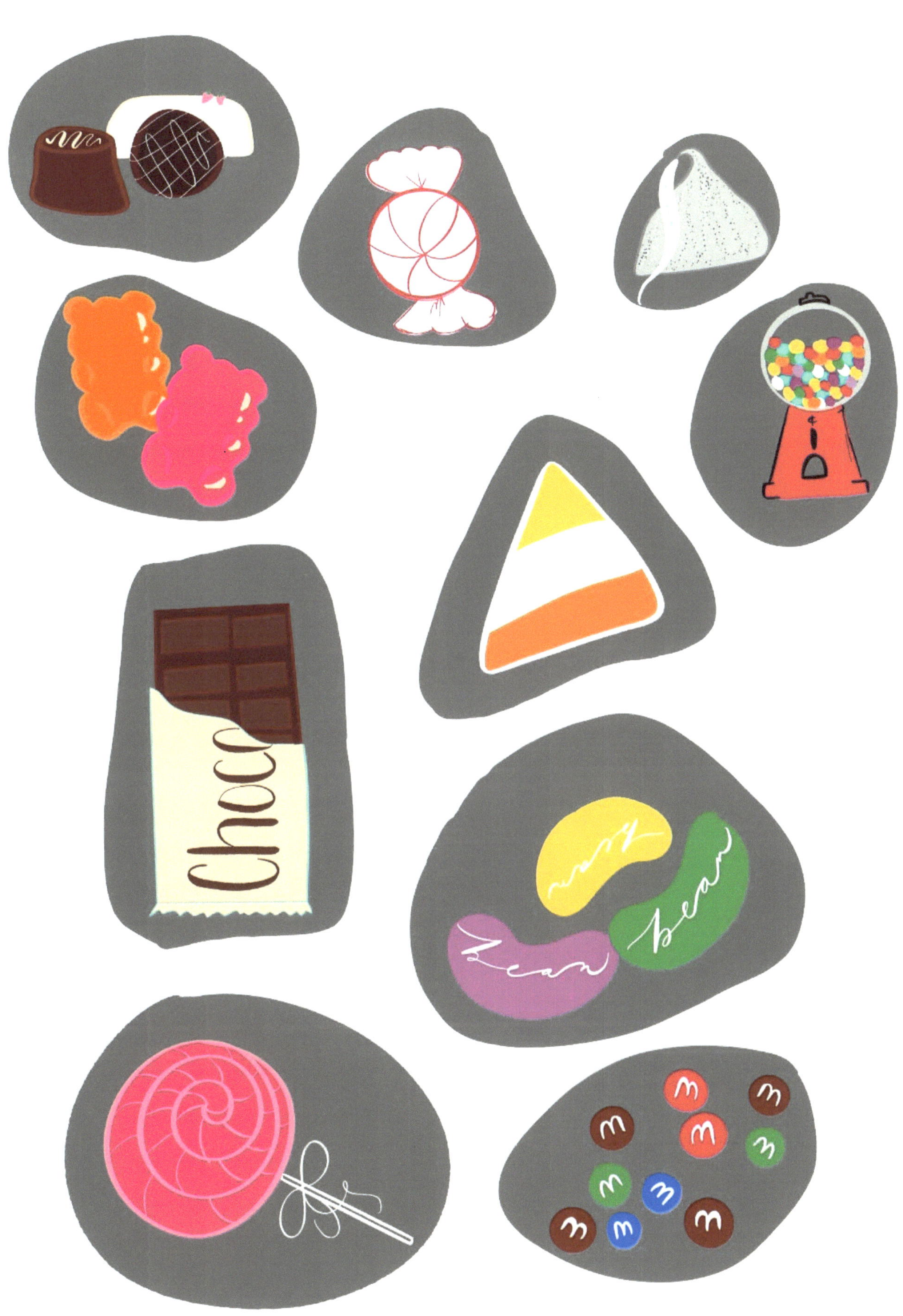

# 1 NEED TO KNOW TIPS

DON'T FORGET - YOU CAN CLEAR COAT YOUR ROCK, THEN ADD DETAILS WITH YOUR MARKERS, AND CLEAR COAT AGAIN WHEN YOU'RE DONE! 🌈 THIS LITTLE TRICK MAKES YOUR COLORS POP EVEN MORE AND KEEPS EVERYTHING SEALED IN BEAUTIFULLY!

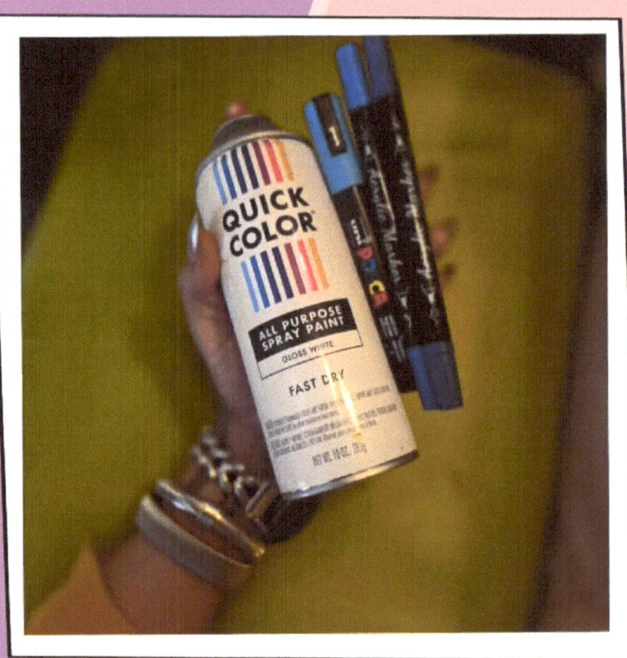


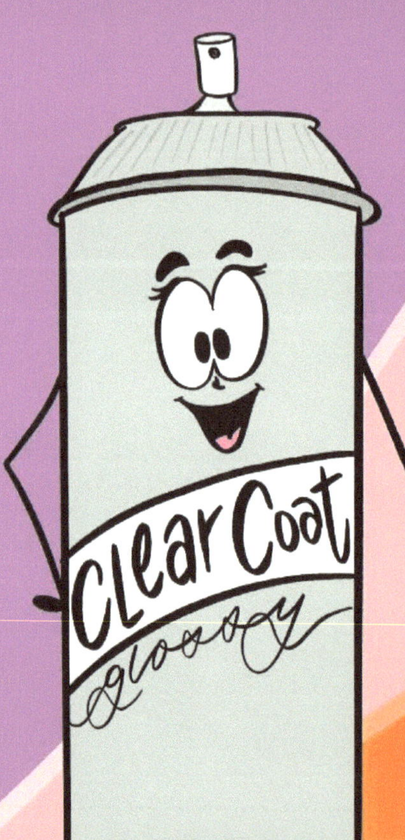


💡 BONUS TIP: IF YOU MAKE A MISTAKE, NO WORRIES! JUST LET YOUR CLEAR COAT DRY AND THEN DRAW RIGHT OVER IT - EASY FIX! 🙌

# 2 NEED TO KNOW TIPS

LET'S TALK ABOUT ONE OF MY FAVORITE THINGS EVER - SUPPLIES! ESPECIALLY ACRYLIC MARKERS 🖊️✨

HONESTLY, BETWEEN WALMART AND AMAZON, I HAVEN'T REALLY FOUND A BRAND I DON'T LIKE! AMAZON USUALLY HAS THE BEST DEALS ON THE BIGGER PACKS, AND IT'S NICE TO HAVE A VARIETY OF COLORS TO PLAY WITH.

A GOOD FINE TIP IS A TOTAL MUST-HAVE - ESPECIALLY IN BLACK AND WHITE FOR OUTLINING AND ADDING DETAILS. I ALSO REALLY LIKE THE DOT TIPS (THEY'RE PERFECT FOR EYES, POLKA DOTS, AND LITTLE ACCENTS!) AND A NICE BRUSH TIP FOR FILLING IN LARGER AREAS SMOOTHLY.

IT REALLY COMES DOWN TO PERSONAL PREFERENCE, SO DON'T BE AFRAID TO TRY A FEW DIFFERENT STYLES AND SEE WHAT FEELS BEST FOR YOU! 💕

I USE ACRYLIC PAINTS AND BRUSHES TOO, BUT MARKERS ARE DEFINITELY MY GO-TO - QUICK, CLEAN, AND SUPER SATISFYING TO WORK WITH! IF YOU EVER WANT TO SPLURGE, POSCA MARKERS ARE ABSOLUTELY AMAZING (BUT YEAH... A LITTLE PRICEY 😅).

🪨💡 PRO TIP: SHAKE YOUR MARKERS WELL BEFORE EACH USE AND TEST THEM ON A SCRAP ROCK OR PAPER FIRST! IT KEEPS THE PAINT FLOWING EVENLY AND HELPS PREVENT BLOTCHES.

WHAT'S YOUR FAVORITE KIND OF MARKER OR BRAND YOU USE FOR YOUR ROCKS? LET'S COMPARE NOTES! 🎨💬

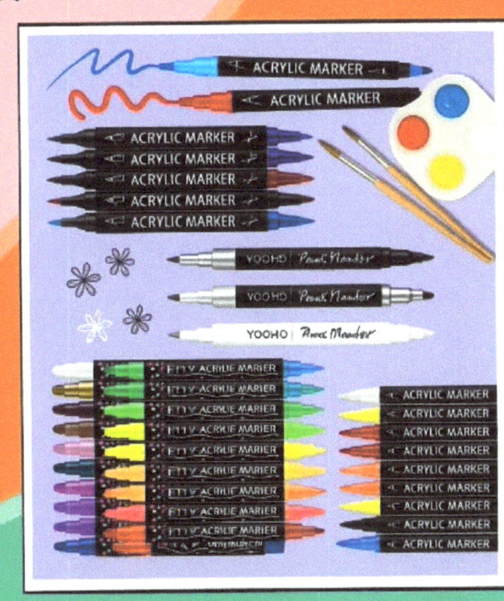

# 3 NEED TO KNOW TIPS

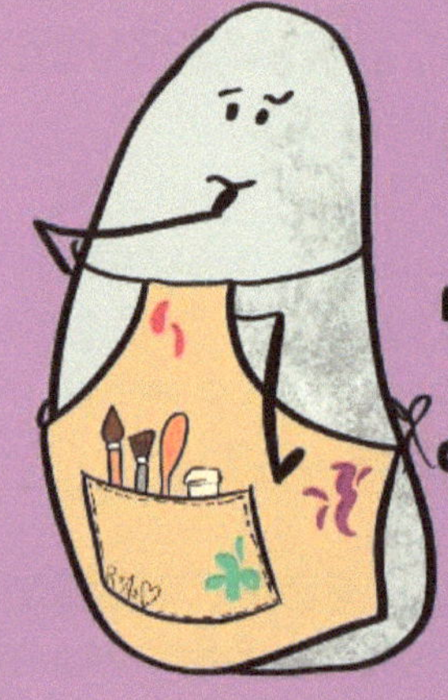

I'VE BEEN FIGHTING WITH THESE TOSHARE 30 COLORS ACRYLIC PAINT PENS (BRAND: SPXKD) ALL DAY - AND I GOTTA SAY, I'M NOT A FAN. THEY CLAIM TO BE "EXTRA FINE TIP" (1MM), BUT NOPE... DEFINITELY NOT! 😂

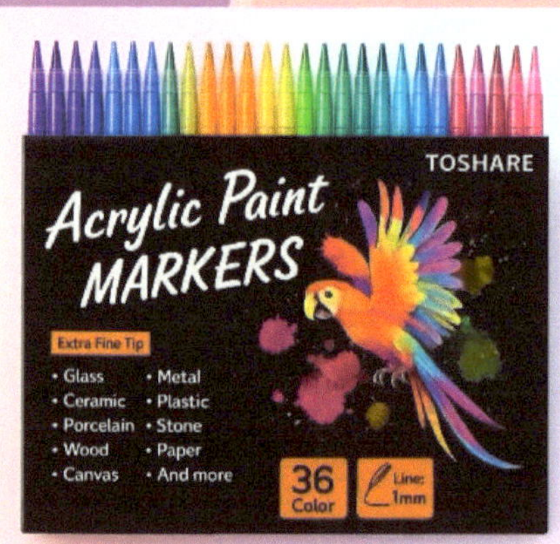


THEY'RE ADVERTISED AS WATERPROOF AND GOOD FOR ROCK PAINTING, CERAMIC, GLASS, WOOD, FABRIC, CANVAS, PORCELAIN, METAL, PUMPKIN CRAFTS - BASICALLY EVERYTHING UNDER THE SUN 🌞 - BUT IN REALITY, THEY JUST DON'T GIVE THAT CLEAN, SMOOTH COVERAGE LIKE I WAS HOPING FOR.

FOR THE PRICE (AROUND $9.99 ON AMAZON), THEY'RE NOT TERRIBLE, BUT IF YOU'RE LOOKING FOR GOOD QUALITY AND ACTUAL FINE DETAIL WORK... SKIP THESE ONES AND SAVE YOURSELF THE HEADACHE!

SOMETIMES THE BEST TIPS COME FROM TRIAL AND ERROR - AND TODAY'S LESSON IS: NOT ALL "FINE TIPS" ARE CREATED EQUAL 🤪

# 4 NEED TO KNOW TIPS

TRUST THE PROCESS! 💪✨ SOMETIMES YOUR ROCK MIGHT LOOK A LITTLE MEH HALFWAY THROUGH - BUT DON'T GIVE UP! KEEP PAINTING, KEEP LAYERING, KEEP ADDING THOSE LITTLE DETAILS... IT ALWAYS COMES TOGETHER IN THE END.

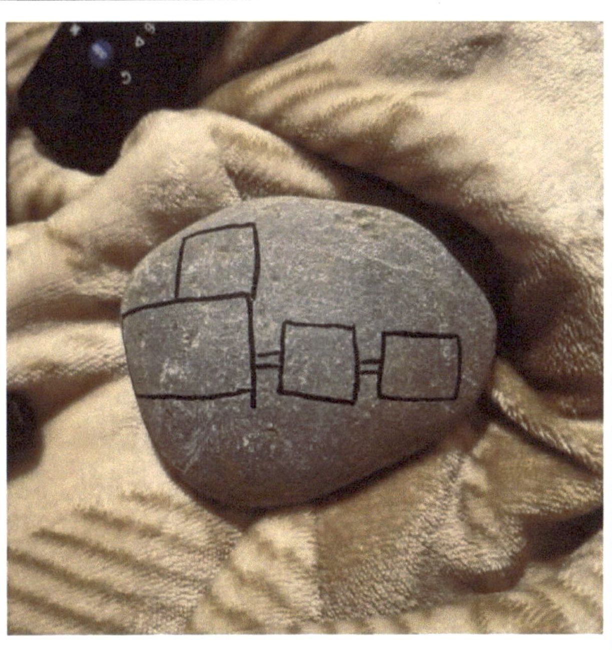

IF YOU DON'T LOVE IT RIGHT AWAY, THAT'S OKAY! YOU CAN FIX ANYTHING WITH PAINT - SERIOUSLY, THAT'S THE BEAUTY OF IT. 🎨🖌️ WHETHER IT'S A SMUDGE, A COLOR YOU REGRET, OR A DESIGN GONE SIDEWAYS, JUST LET IT DRY, PAINT OVER IT, AND START AGAIN.

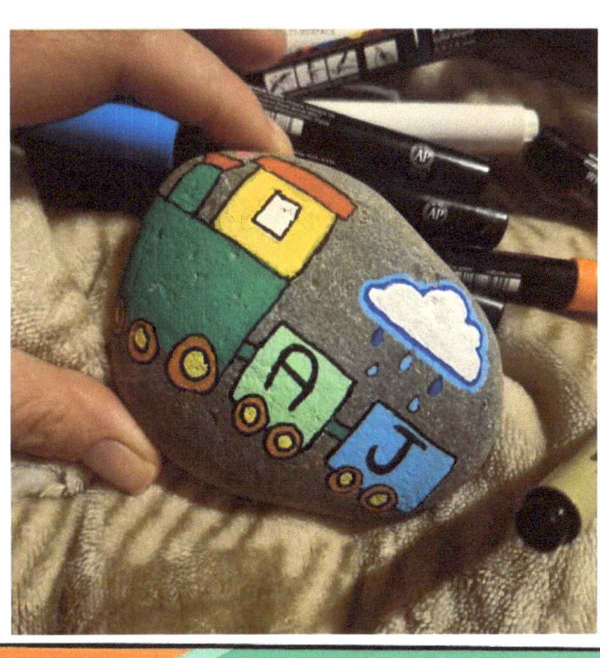


MOST IMPORTANTLY - DON'T STRESS! THIS IS SUPPOSED TO BE FUN, RELAXING, AND CREATIVE. 💕 EVERY ROCK IS A LEARNING EXPERIENCE, AND EACH ONE MAKES YOU A LITTLE BETTER THAN THE LAST.

KEEP PAINTING, KEEP SMILING, AND REMEMBER - THE ONLY "MISTAKE" IS QUITTING TOO SOON! 🪨💖

OKAY FRIENDS, THIS ONE'S SUPER IMPORTANT IF YOU WANT YOUR BEAUTIFUL ROCKS TO SURVIVE THE WEATHER – SEAL THEM! 💦☀️❄️

AFTER ALL THAT HARD WORK PAINTING, THE LAST THING YOU WANT IS YOUR COLORS FADING OR WASHING AWAY. I ALWAYS SEAL MINE ONCE THEY'RE FULLY DRY, AND MY GO-TO IS THIS ONE RIGHT HERE 👉 KRYLON TRIPLE THICK CRYSTAL CLEAR GLAZE! 🙌

IT GIVES YOUR ROCKS THAT SHINY, GLASS-LIKE FINISH AND REALLY MAKES THE COLORS POP! PLUS, IT DRIES QUICK AND HOLDS UP AMAZING OUTDOORS. 🌈

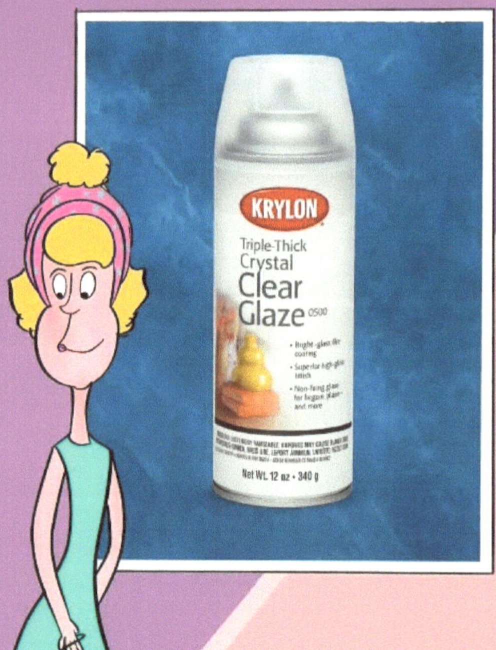


💡 QUICK TIP:

MAKE SURE YOUR PAINT IS COMPLETELY DRY BEFORE SEALING.

SPRAY IN LIGHT, EVEN COATS (OUTSIDE OR IN A WELL-VENTILATED AREA).

LET IT DRY BETWEEN COATS FOR THE BEST FINISH!

TRUST ME – THIS STEP IS SO WORTH IT! YOUR ROCKS WILL LOOK EXTRA GLOSSY AND STAY GORGEOUS WAY LONGER. 💕

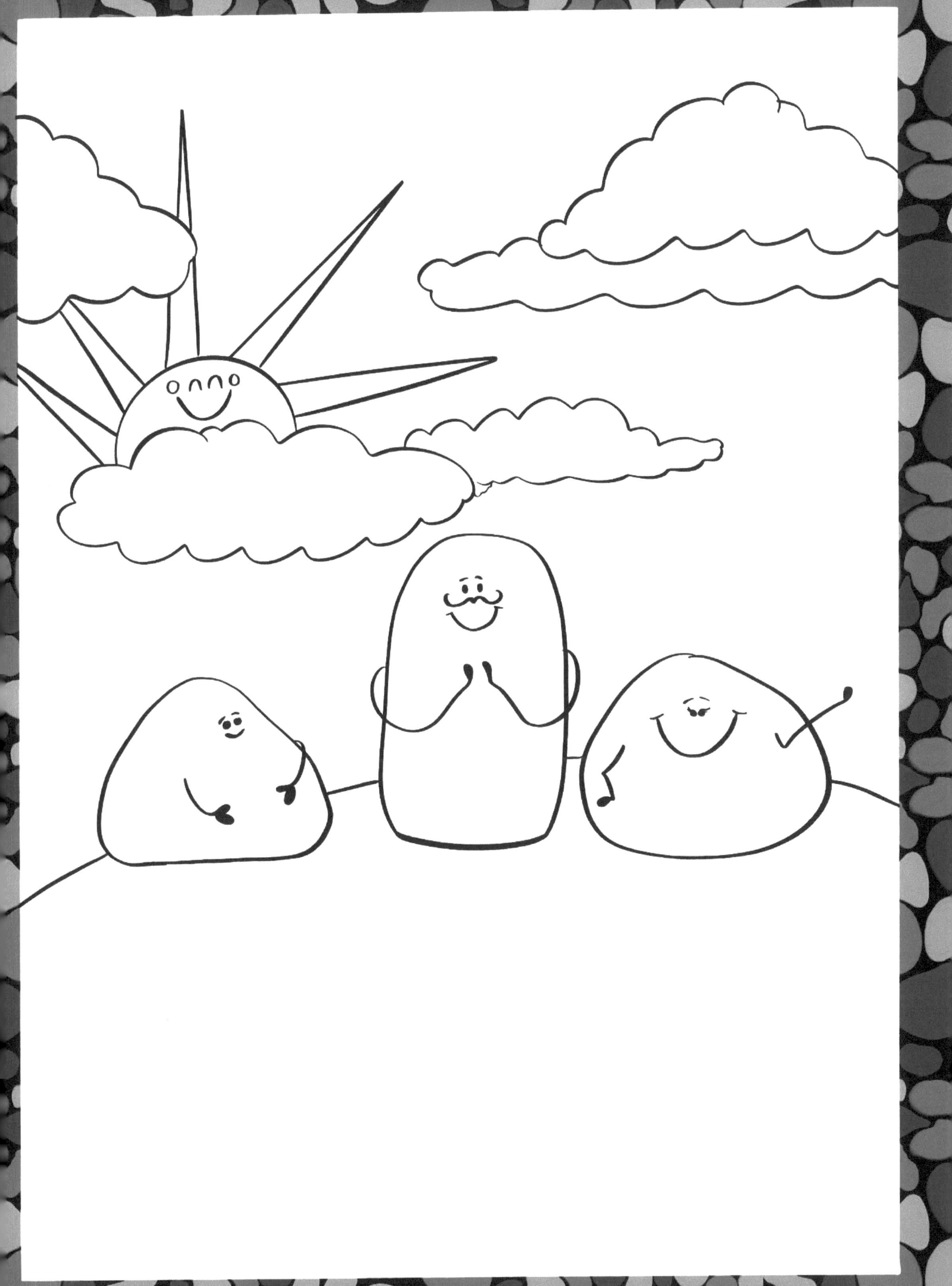

# PRACTICE ROCKS

A PERFECT PLACE TO PRACTICE BEFORE YOU PAINT!
YOU CAN ALSO DRAW YOUR IDEAS TO SAVE FOR LATER.

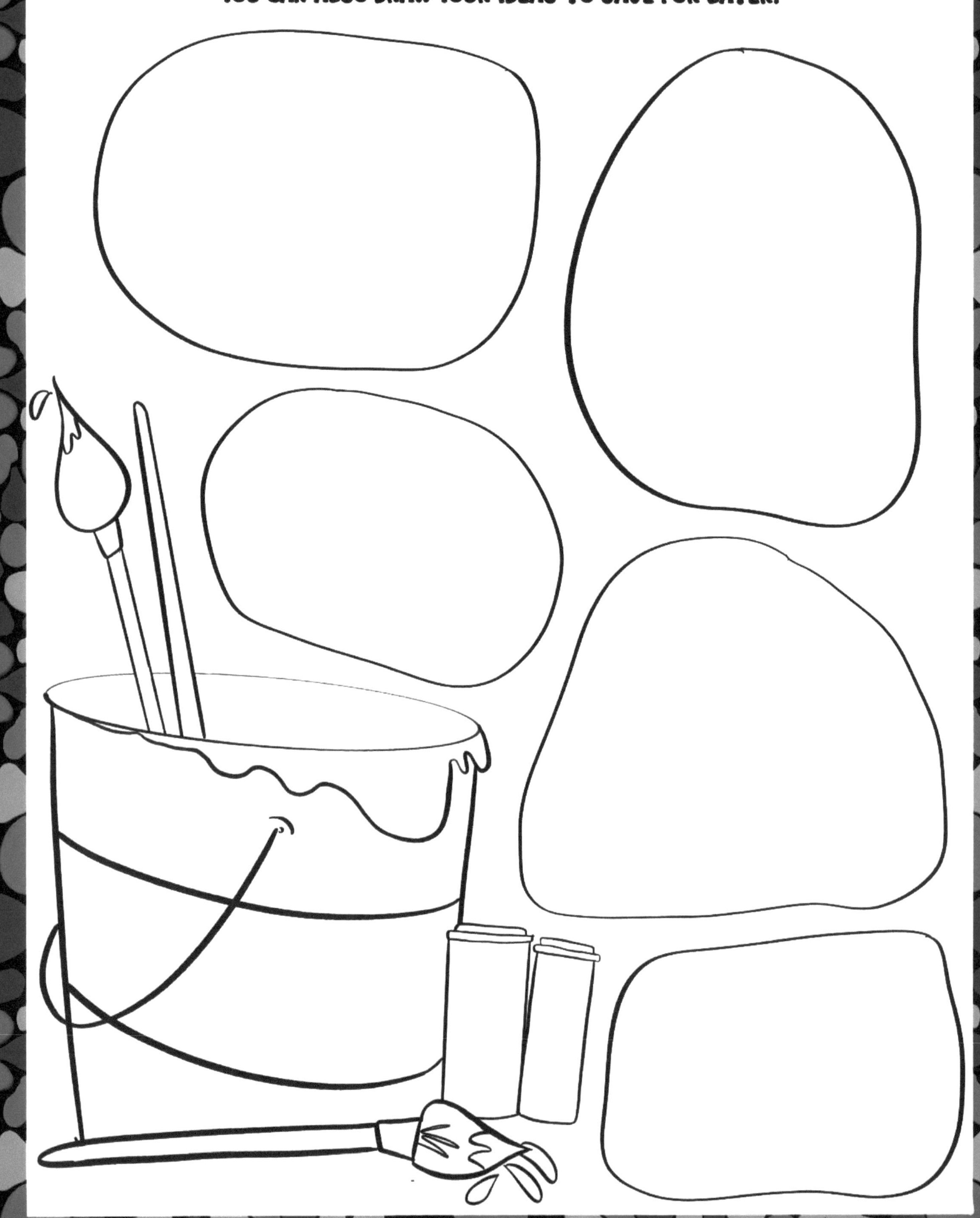

# DRESS ME UP

I NEED A NEW LOOK FOR A BIRTHDAY PARTY.
CAN YOU HELP?

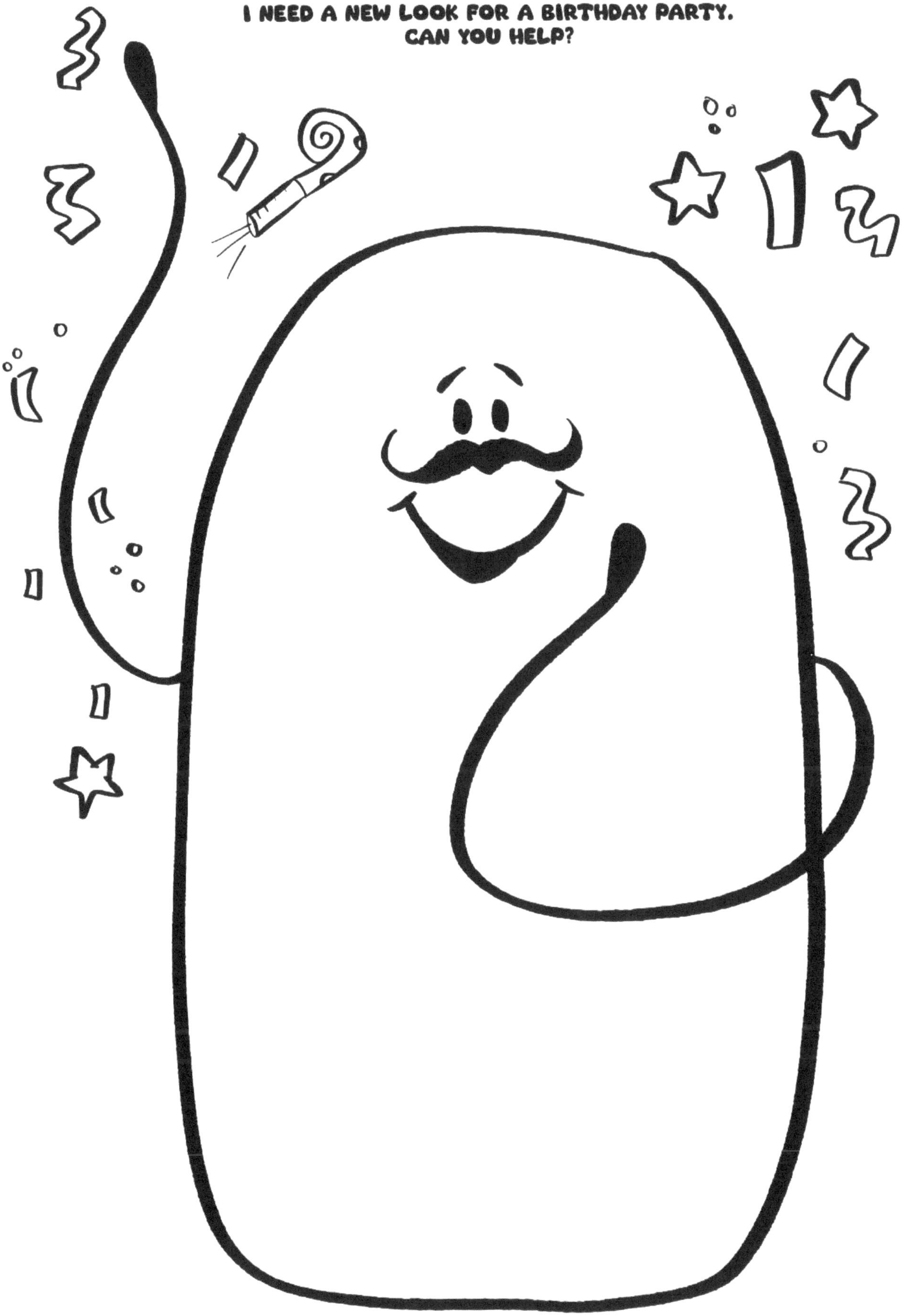

# DRESS ME UP

I HAVE A COSTUME PARTY TO GO TO.
WHAT SHOULD I GO AS?

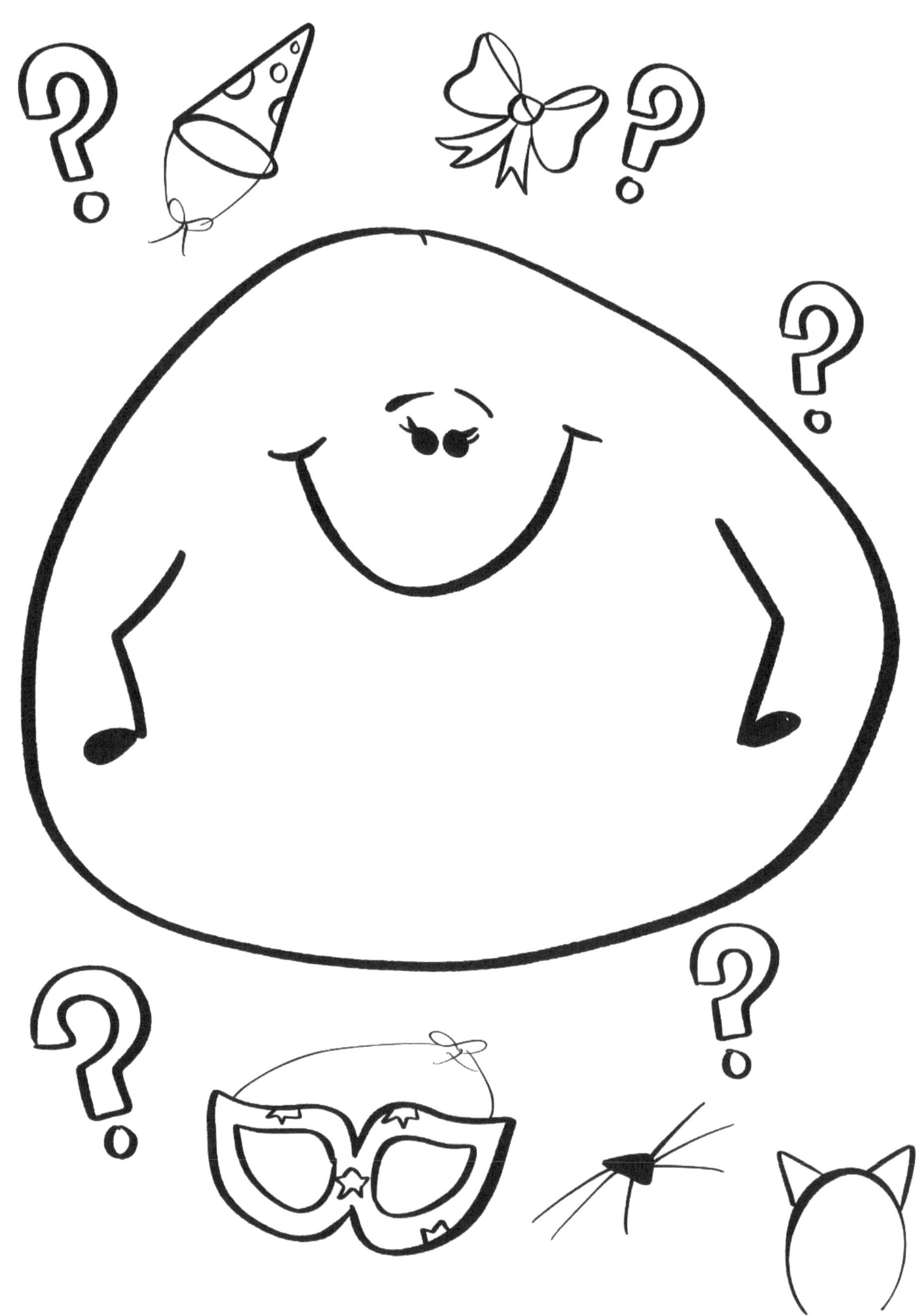

# DRESS ME UP

**IT'S MY FIRST DAY OF MY NEW JOB!**
**CAN YOU HELP ME PICK OUT THE PERFECT OUTFIT?**

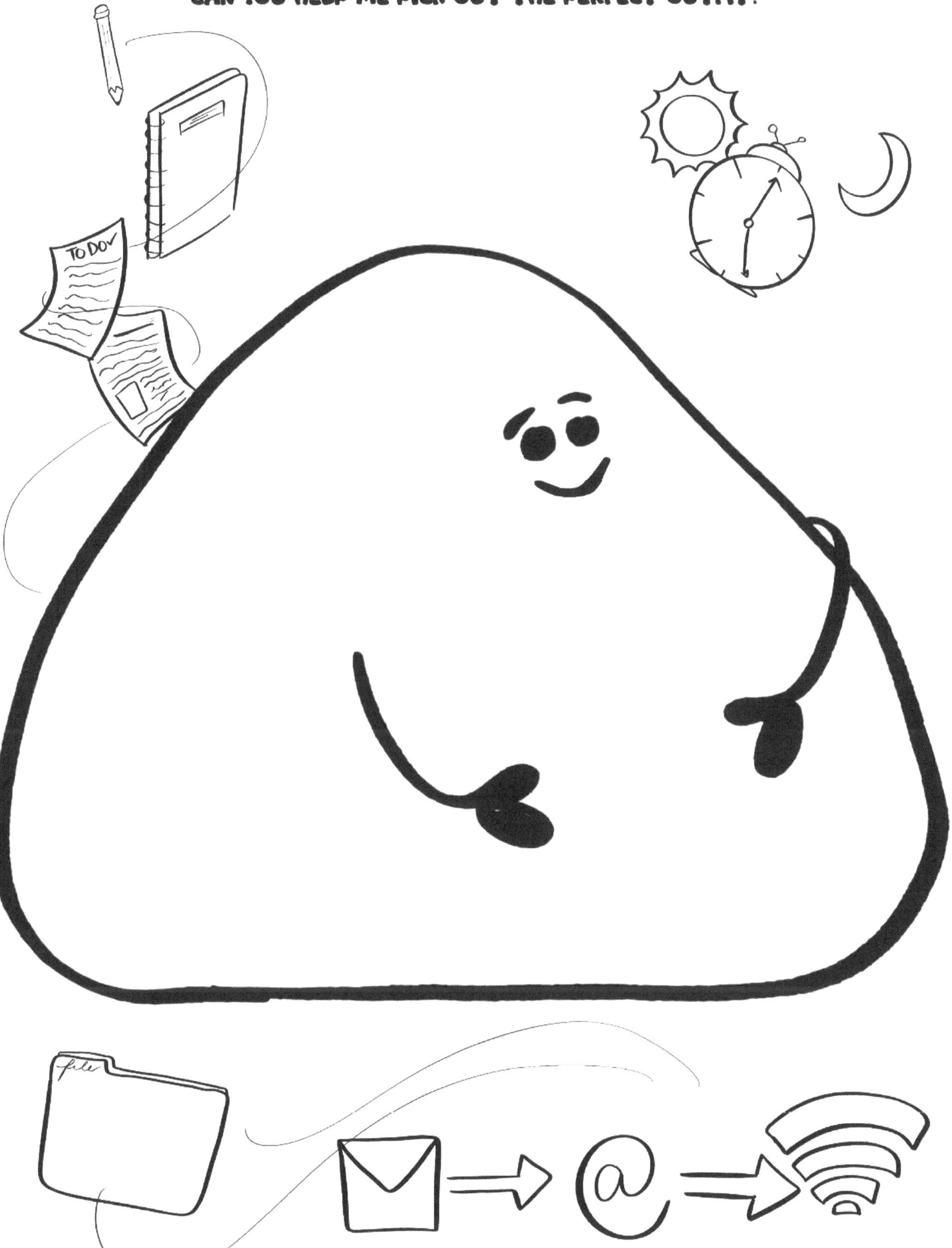

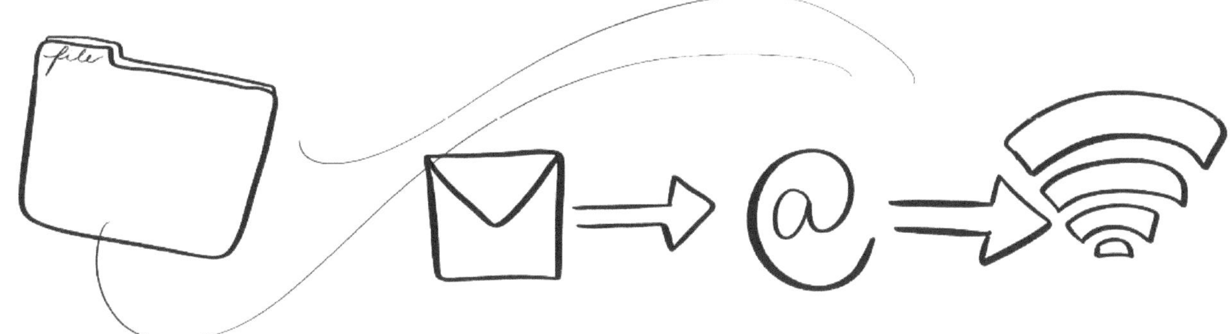

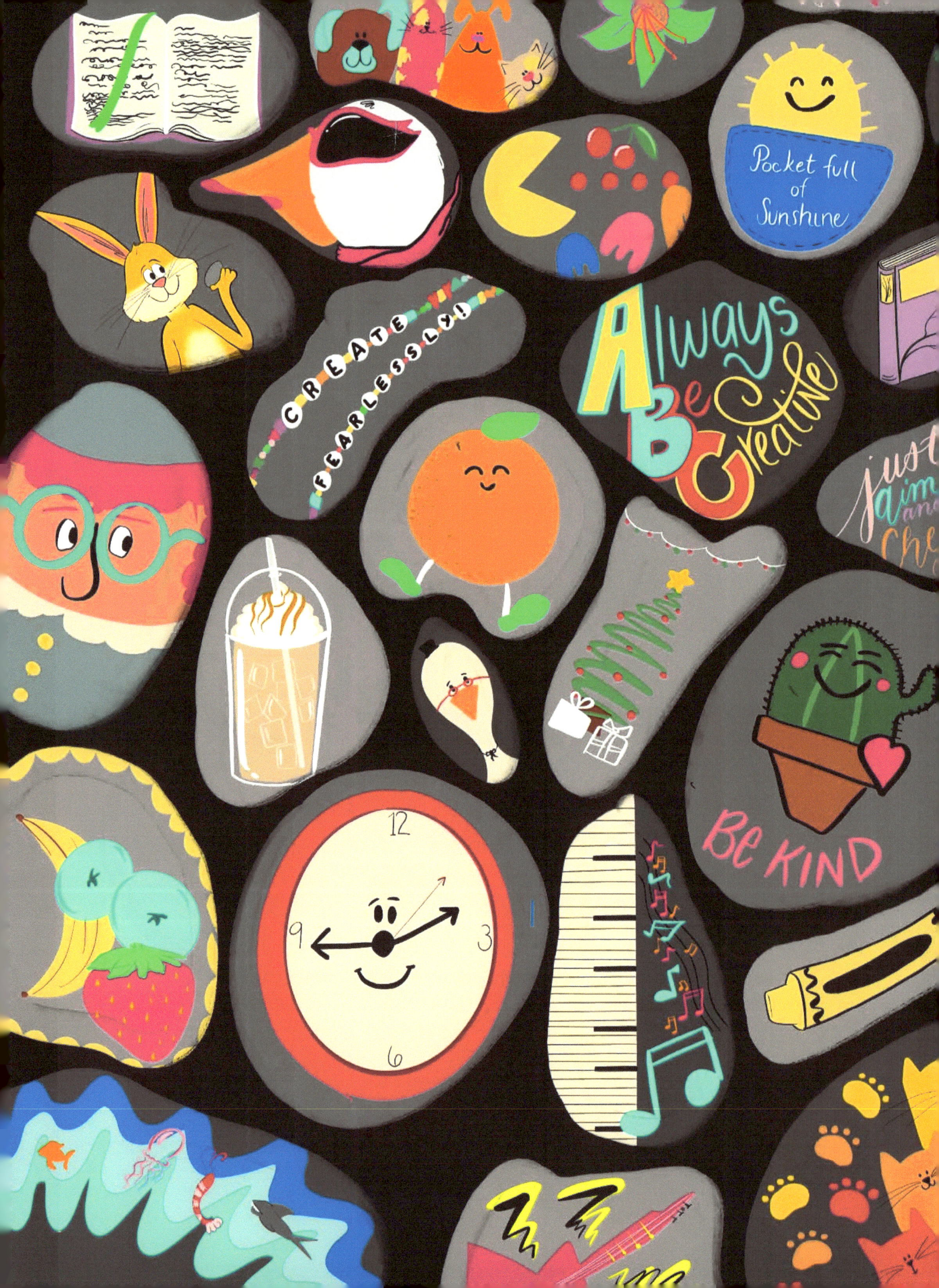
Pocket full of Sunshine
CREATE FEARLESSLY!
Always Be Creative
12
9
3
6
Be KIND

www.ingramcontent.com/pod-product-compliance
Ingram Content Group UK Ltd.
Pitfield, Milton Keynes, MK11 3LW, UK
UKHW060120300726
14090UKWH00002B/290

* 9 7 8 1 9 6 9 9 2 6 0 7 5 *